Coping with

ALLERGIES

Peter M. G. Deane, M.D.
and Robert H. Schwartz, M.D.

THE ROSEN PUBLISHING GROUP, INC./NEW YORK

Published in 1999 by The Rosen Publishing Group, Inc.
29 East 21st Street, New York, NY 10010

First Edition

Cover photo by Thaddeus Harden

Library of Congress Cataloging-in-Publication Data

Schwartz, Robert H.
    Coping with allergies / by Robert H. Schwartz and Peter M.G. Deane.
        p.   cm. — (Coping)
    Includes bibliographical references and index.
    Summary: Offers information on the symptoms, diagnosis, and treatment of the most common types of allergies, as well as some non-medical ways to manage allergies.
    ISBN 0-8239-2511-0
    1. Allergy Juvenile literature. [1. Allergy.]   I. Deane, Peter M.G.
II. Title. III. Series.
    RC584.S39 1999
    616.97—dc21   99-33842
                                                                          CIP

Manufactured in the United States of America

About the Authors

Dr. Robert H. Schwartz is a board-certified practitioner of pediatric allergy and allergy immunology. After completing his under-graduate education at Dartmouth College, Dr. Schwartz graduated with honors from the University of Rochester School of Medicine and Dentistry in Rochester, New York. In 1985 he cofounded Allergy, Asthma, Immunology of Rochester (AAIR), a medical prac-tice and research center. Dr. Schwartz is the author of more than 150 medical papers, book chapters, and scientific abstracts, as well as editor-in-chief of the journal *Pediatric Asthma, Allergy, and Immunology.* He is a former director of the American Board of Allergy and Immunology and the Rochester Cystic Fibrosis Care Teaching and Resource Center. Currently Dr. Schwartz is clinical professor of pediatrics and codirector of the Allergy and Immunology Training Program at the University of Rochester Medical Center. A resident of Rochester, he is married and the father of two daughters.

Dr. Peter Michael Grace Deane is a board-certified practitioner of internal medicine and rheumatology, and for the care of children and adults with allergic diseases. He received his undergraduate education at the University of Pennsylvania and his medical degree at the University of Rochester School of Medicine and Dentistry, where he graduated with honors. He is clinical assistant professor of medicine and emergency medicine at the University of Rochester School of Medicine and Dentistry.

To Kate and Robbie, with love.

—PMGD

In the memory of Emanuel Schwartz, M.D.
1901–1969
Allergist, 1945–1969.

—RHS

Contents

Introduction

Everyone knows what it's like to have a pimple or blemish on one's nose. It is a common problem. Friends may laugh and others may smile when they see you with a zit. But for you, this is serious. You might be embarrassed. You may not want to be seen. You may wonder how it got there. You hope there will not be more. You pray that it clears up before your date on Friday. You stay home. You worry that you might have some chronic skin disease. You want it to go away as fast as possible. These feelings, thoughts, worries, and hopes are similar to what people with allergies have. Perhaps you are one of these people as well.

Allergy is a term coined in 1906 by Dr. Clemens Von Pirquet. He was a highly respected pediatrician who became the first chairman of the Department of Pediatrics at the famous Johns Hopkins Hospital in Baltimore, Maryland. Dr. Von Pirquet wrote, "I propose the term Allergy. 'Allos' implies deviation from the original state, from the behavior of the normal individual...." If you think this is confusing, imagine how people felt close to 100 years ago!

Allergy means changed reactivity. In very simple terms, an allergy is an unusual sensitivity to a substance that normally does not affect most people. This sensitivity is due to some kind of change in your immune system, which overreacts in response. (This is very different from an immune deficiency, such as the disease known as AIDS, or acquired immune deficiency syndrome, which is characterized by an immune system that underreacts.)

Today, the noun "allergy" and the adjective "allergic" are a common part of our daily language. We use these terms frequently and casually, often with a smile, as a metaphor to describe threats from things, agents, or people that provoke or annoy us—for instance, "I'm allergic to my teacher."

But this kind of loose talk contributes to our failure to recognize the very real discomfort felt by the more than 50 million Americans who suffer from allergic conditions. Allergy can be very serious. For instance, each year, approximately 5,000 people in the United States die from asthma, a breathing problem affecting 5 percent of the population that is usually caused by allergic mechanisms.

So today, the word "allergy" deserves some respect, not only because it is common and can be serious but also because of the following:

⇀ We know a lot about what allergy is.

⇀ We know what causes allergy.

⇀ We know how it happens.

⇀ We know what to do about it.

More important, because today's doctors and scientists are discovering new things about allergy and are making new medicines to treat allergies, tomorrow's sufferers will surely have the knowledge and tools to prevent allergies and completely control them.

So allergy is a common problem, and a serious one for many people. "Allergy" as a concept translates to many different illnesses, including asthma, hay fever, sinus infections, insect sting allergy, food allergy, medication allergy, and others! Each of these can be mild for one person and terribly severe for the next. Some people have only one problem from this list; some have several. If you do not know what all of these are, that's okay. That means you probably do not have those particular problems. And you will know all about them by the end of this book.

Many patients with allergies find that dealing with their illness(es) is much easier if they know as much as they possibly can about what is wrong with them. This book was written to help you do just that. It will cover all these illnesses. We will discuss their causes, courses, and treatments. Precisely because the causes of allergic diseases are external, knowledge about them is often very powerful. You can have control over the cause, and therefore over the illness itself. This is not true for most diseases. With allergies, sometimes you can remove the cause—and the illness with it. This means that although you may be allergic to something, you may not have to be sick from it.

Even in cases where you cannot remove the causes, treatments have become easier, safer, and more effective than ever. The pace at which new treatments are appearing is faster, too. One specialty of physicians—allergists—exists just to care for patients with allergies and to keep up with the ever-changing research and treatments. The wide variety of treatments will also be covered in this book. If you know more about what ails you, you will feel better about yourself and your treatment. You will feel more in control. And that will help you get on with your life.

Asthma and Allergy by the Numbers

➷ Fifty million Americans have asthma or allergies.

➷ Thirty-five million Americans have hay fever (seasonal allergic rhinitis).

➷ Fifteen million Americans have asthma; five million of these are children.

➷ Almost twelve million Americans are affected by the following allergic conditions:

⊙ Eczema

⊙ Urticaria (hives)

⊙ Angioedema (swelling)

⊙ Allergic reactions to food, medications, or insect stings

➷ One in five children seen by a pediatrician has a major allergic disorder.

➷ Seven percent of all children in the United States have asthma.

➥ Allergies tend to run in families. If one parent is allergic, the child has a one in four chance of developing an allergy. If both parents are allergic, it is likely two out of three children will be allergic also.

➥ In 1990, there were 4,600 deaths in the United States from asthma. Today, the vast majority of asthmatics are able to have their disease effectively controlled by medication and treatment.

➥ In 1988 in the United States, there were 15 million visits to physicians for asthma. Thirty-five percent of these patients were younger than twenty.

➥ Ten percent of Americans suffer from asthma or frequent wheezing at some point in their lives.

➥ Seventy-five percent of asthma sufferers experience exercise-induced asthma.

➥ Those at greatest risk of death from asthma are persons older than fifty and those younger than nine.

➥ Asthma is the most common cause of admissions to most children's hospitals.

➥ Allergies are the sixth-leading cause of chronic disease in the United States.

➥ Slightly more than one out of every five (21 percent) children with asthma in the United States was hospitalized in 1988.

⇨ In the United States, 48 percent of children with asthma have to be taken to an emergency room to be treated for an asthma attack at some point.

⇨ According to the U.S. Centers for Disease Control, reports of asthma have risen 75 percent since 1980. Asthma has increased 160 percent among children.

⇨ One-half of asthmatics are female. Asthma complicates pregnancy one percent of the time. When asthmatics are pregnant, approximately one-third have fewer symptoms, one-third become worse, and one-third remain the same.

⇨ African Americans with asthma are about three times as likely to die of asthma as are whites.

⇨ Each year in the United States, 35 million days are spent in bed as a result of asthma.

⇨ Twenty-eight million days of restricted activity, 6 million days of bed rest, 3.5 million days of work loss, 2 million lost school days, and 8.4 million office visits are experienced annually by hay fever sufferers in the United States.

⇨ Six million children in the United States have hay fever.

⇨ Two million children in the United States have eczema (atopic dermatitis).

↪ A reported fifty deaths result each year in the United States from insect stings, with many more deaths going unreported.

↪ Recent estimates indicate that nearly 200,000 Americans suffer allergic drug reactions each year while in the hospital, and 50,000 more Americans are hospitalized because of allergic reactions to drugs.

The Dollars and Cents of Allergies

↪ Americans suffering from asthma spend $6.2 billion each year, including $1.6 billion on hospital care and $1 billion on asthma medications.

↪ Retail sales of over-the-counter allergy relief medications totaled $1.5 billion in the United States in 1994, and market researchers estimated an increase by more than $1.2 billion in 1999.

↪ A recent examination of insurance claims filed in the United States over a three-month period showed that chronic asthmatics filed for more than $33 million in treatment costs.

↪ Hay fever sufferers in the United States spend $225 million annually on physician services and $297 million on drugs.

What Are Allergies?

Our immune system serves to protect us from infections. Normally this means that it keeps us well. But if your immune system begins to react against something you inhale, eat, or get on your skin—something that itself is not harmful—this can be the beginning of an allergic illness. The substance could be as seemingly insignificant as a pollen grain, a peanut, or a dust mite. What scientists believe happens is that the body of the person who is allergic reacts as if this substance is from an invading parasite.

Before the development of modern methods of sanitation, unpleasant creatures such as hookworms were regular invaders of our bodies. In some countries today, parasites are still a major problem, but in the United States we have pretty much eliminated them (except for a few problems like pinworm) as a public health hazard. But the human immune system remains on the lookout for these invaders. When it senses one, it makes specific proteins called antibodies, which attach to the foreign substances. There are five different types of antibodies, and the arm of the immune system involved in allergic reactions makes a specific type—known as immunoglobulin E, or IgE—found in parasitic and allergic diseases. These antibodies bind to the foreign material and activate the action of white blood cells, which guard against infection.

When certain people inhale common pollen grains, as from grass or ragweed, or animal dander (dried skin secretions), their immune system responds to defend them. This occurs even though pollen grains and dander, by themselves, cannot do anything harmful to our bodies. Scientists do not know why some people's immune systems react to these specific things as dangerous. But allergic antibodies are made, and white blood cells then go to the site of the immune reaction. The tissues there swell and water. When this takes place in our eyes and nose, we get the watery eyes and stuffy, runny nose of hay fever. The effect is somewhat different in other parts of our body, such as our lungs and bowels, but the basic reaction is the same.

When the white blood cells reach our tissues, they make lots of chemicals that help us resist infection. Some of those chemicals are so well known that they have medicines named after them. Histamine makes fluid leak from our blood vessels, and it makes the nerves that control itching go crazy. Sound like a nose you know? If so, maybe you have taken an antihistamine for hay fever. If you have asthma, you may have heard of a new class of medications that block the effects of leukotrienes, which are cellular compounds generated by the allergic response. There are also cells in our bodies that try to control our immune responses with cortisone and other steroids (substances produced naturally by the body, as opposed to the anabolic steroids used by athletes for bodybuilding, which generally are synthetic hormones).

Many Problems Are Not Allergies

If allergies are unnecessary immune reactions to things that are not dangerous to us, then many of the problems we refer to as allergies are not. You cannot be allergic to your sister. You cannot be "allergic to the twentieth century."

You can be allergic to something you smell or eat, but you cannot be allergic to something the first time you smell it or eat it. You have to be exposed to something once for your immune system to make you allergic to it. This is true for pollen as well as for foods, medications, and insect stings.

Some things are just plain toxic, or poisonous. Bees and wasps inject venom when they sting, so there is usually some reaction at the site where you are stung. Such local reactions are to be expected. Some medications are both safe and effective at appropriate doses, but if taken in too high a dose may be poisonous, with any number of bad effects.

Many medicines have side effects. For example, many aspirin-like medicines, including ibuprofen, can cause stomach upset, which leads people to say, "I'm allergic to aspirin." Not so. They just cannot tolerate its effect on their stomachs, so they should not use it. While side effects are often predictable, allergies are not. Side effects are often dose-related: The more of something you take, the more effect it has on you. Allergies are not dose-related: If you have allergic antibodies to something, exposure to even a small amount will set off an allergic reaction.

Many foods bother people. Some people cannot digest milk sugar (lactose) and therefore are bothered by dairy foods. Fatty foods give some people diarrhea. Alcohol is notorious for stomach upset and headache, but some cheeses can also give people "hangovers." We treated a patient who told us, "I'm very allergic to chocolate. Whenever I eat it I get angry." This may seem funny, but chocolate really did bother this person. He just was not allergic to it in the medical sense.

Some foods, such as red wine or chocolate, can give people headaches and can even trigger migraine headaches. Migraines are sometimes said to be a kind of allergic problem, but they are not. They are triggered by problems in the blood vessels in the brain. Many other ailments are often said to be allergic but are not. Of all the kinds of arthritis, none are allergic. Lupus is not caused by allergies. Neither is psoriasis.

Headaches from sinus problems, as well as a runny and stuffy nose, certainly can be caused by hay fever. We will cover the major allergic diseases in this book, but listen carefully for the times when people say they are allergic to something—it's amazing how often the word is tossed around incorrectly.

Can You Catch an Allergy?

If you are allergic, there is a very good chance that your parents were allergic, too.

But wait a second. What do we mean by "allergic" here?

When scientists study people with allergic diseases, they find that there are three diseases that are truly "allergic": hay fever, asthma, and the skin problem known as atopic dermatitis (which means "allergic skin inflammation"). These three ailments seem to be related, both in the allergens that cause them and in the sort of response the body makes to those allergens.

17

So what is the chance of inheriting allergies from your parents? Genetically, it is no simple matter, like eye color. There are many genetic factors involved, probably about a dozen. But your chances of being allergic are definitely increased if your parents are allergic. Someone in the general population has about a 20 percent chance of having an allergic disease. If one parent is allergic, the chance increases to 50 percent. If both parents are allergic, it rises to 70 percent. And if both parents are allergic, allergic problems are likely to start in early childhood, often before the second birthday. Allergies often start years later in those with one or no allergic parents.

This genetic predisposition holds true for allergic disease in general, but not for any one disease in particular. For example, both parents may have hay fever, and their child may have only atopic dermatitis. So, you cannot truly say that you have inherited your mother's asthma, for example.

We also know that if you have one allergic disease, you are at higher risk for others. Hay fever and asthma often go together, and the hay fever often seems to start first. Some children seem to march from one illness to the next: atopic dermatitis as a baby, then hay fever a few years later as the skin condition improves with age. Then asthma develops as the child grows even older.

What about medication and insect sting allergies? These seem to be simply the (bad) luck of the draw. You might hear a person say, "I'm allergic to penicillin because my mother was." Not so. As hard as scientists have looked for it, there seems to be no hereditary involvement in allergy to medication. And remember, if someone has never had penicillin, he or she cannot be allergic to it.

One conclusion to be drawn from these facts is that 30 percent of people with two allergic parents never develop allergies. Why not? There must be something around, or something not around, that influences whether we become allergic at all. Only after that do our bodies decide to what we will be allergic.

Several things have been shown to be important influences on whether our bodies become allergic. Let's discuss them one at a time.

Cigarette Smoke

Why would anyone in his or her right mind smoke? The answer, in part, is that nicotine is fiercely addictive. None of the chemicals in tobacco smoke are good for you, though, and they promote allergy in several ways. Adult smokers and their children (who by being exposed to cigarette smoke become what is known as passive smokers) make more allergic-type antibodies. Children of smoking mothers are four times more likely to develop an allergic disease by eighteen months of age. They more frequently develop atopic dermatitis. They more frequently and earlier develop hay fever and asthma. They get more middle ear infections. The risk to children increases with smoking during pregnancy and after pregnancy.

Dust Mite Exposure

High levels of these tiny creatures in the bedding of children younger than one leads to vigorous production of dust mite-specific antibodies in small children. These same children are 4.8 times more likely to have asthma by age eleven.

Cats

Children less than one year old with cats in their homes have an increased chance of developing asthma by their teenage years.

Cockroaches

Evidence is now emerging that these pests are as detrimental as dust mites and cats in the development of allergies.

Infections

You might be surprised to learn that infections have no clear role in the development of any allergic disease. The research on the topic is greatly complicated by the fact that all children get a number of colds. More children are in day care than ever before, and they get more infections (including middle ear infections), but not more allergic diseases. Or so it seems right now.

Food or Food Avoidance

Medical researchers have been looking at this question for many years. Avoiding certain foods (such as dairy products, peanuts, eggs, and soy) during pregnancy seems not to prevent the development of allergies in children. Avoiding them during breast-feeding does not help either. Neither does breast-feeding, as opposed to bottle-feeding. Some people advocate avoiding certain foods for small children (peanuts, fish) but there is no solid proof that this prevents allergies either.

A common theme here is the role played by exposure to potential allergens in the first year of life. The immune system apparently decides in the first year of life whether to be allergic or not. The critical early allergens appear to be cockroaches, dust mites, and cats. Later on, the allergic response broadens to include other things, such as pollens. Exposure to cigarette smoke is like adding gas to the fire.

Allergic Ailments

At this point, a brief description of the common allergic diseases we will be discussing in this book may be helpful.

Hay Fever
Hay fever, which is sometimes called sinusitis, is the classic allergic disease. It is what people are most often referring to when they say they have "allergies." Stuffy nose, postnasal drip, sneezing, and itching in the ears, nose, and throat are typical symptoms. Many just have it in the spring (it is sometimes called "rose fever" because that is when roses bloom) or in the fall ("hay fever" because it occurs at haying time). Some people may have no seasonal pattern to their symptoms; for others, symptoms may peak in any season. Winter is virus season, which partly explains why winter is also sinusitis season. Eye problems commonly accompany nose symptoms and for some people are the worst part. The eyes get red, itchy, and watery, too, which makes the nose runnier.

Asthma
When we breathe, air enters our body through the nose

and mouth, moves through the throat and voice box, and flows on into the lungs. In a person with asthma, the lungs' air passages become red and irritated. They cannot feel pain, but when irritated they trigger coughing. The airways' muscular walls twitch and spasm (tighten up without letting go). The airways produce mucus, which clogs things up. These factors together make it very hard to move air in and out. So we feel short of breath or like our chest is tight. Air whistles through the now-tiny breathing passages, a phenomenon we often refer to as "wheezing." For some, asthma is an intermittent problem; for others it comes on with exercise and cold air. For those with severe asthma, it may attack every night, replacing rest with the suffocating feeling of not getting enough air.

Anaphylaxis

Sorry to get technical, but the term is important. An attack of anaphylaxis is a whole-body allergic reaction: skin and lungs and bowels and blood pressure. If you hear that someone died of an allergic reaction, it was probably because of anaphylaxis induced by whatever it was to which they were allergic. It could be a peanut or venom from a yellow jacket sting or penicillin. The resulting illness is sudden and life-threatening. People who have experienced anaphylaxis may wear identification bracelets so that they never receive a certain medication, or they may carry a syringe of adrenaline with which to inject themselves if they are exposed to a substance that has caused anaphylaxis (from a bee sting, for example).

Insect Sting Allergy

Many insects bite: mosquitoes, flies, and so on. They "bite" in the sense that they attack us with their mouths. Bees, wasps (including yellow jackets), and fire ants ("red ants") are the insects that sting us. These creatures all inject venom through their stingers. This venom causes local reactions, which get worse with a greater number of stings. But even one sting can cause an anaphylactic reaction in a person who is allergic to the venom.

Medication Allergy

If you consult a medication reference book, such as the *Physicians' Desk Reference*, you will see that virtually everything listed can cause an allergic reaction. Such reactions can range from mild or severe rashes all the way to anaphylaxis. Penicillin is the classic example of a medication that can trigger such reactions, but sulfa drugs, aspirin-type drugs, and medicines for seizures are also common causes. Physicians understand penicillin allergy the best and know how to test for it. This is helpful not just because avoiding a reaction is obviously good for patients, but because penicillin allergy may fade over time. Thus, patients who have experienced penicillin allergy may, in time, be able to use penicillin and penicillin-type antibiotics effectively and safely.

Food Allergies

In theory, anyone can become allergic to any food, but this usually does not happen. From our tonsils on down, our immune systems know what we eat. They actively decide not to react to our foods. Even so, occasionally we become allergic to a food, for reasons that are unknown. Common examples of foods that cause an allergic reaction are peanuts and shellfish. The allergic reaction people can experience from food ranges from a few hives to full-blown anaphylaxis. Nausea, vomiting, and diarrhea without other symptoms are rarely due to a food allergy. They are more likely to be due to food intolerance or even food poisoning.

Hives

These shifting, itchy patches on the skin can come by the pair or by the dozen. They can also be a frustrating mystery for patient and doctor alike. Many times people figure out what caused their hives by thinking about their previous meal: "That's right, I had shrimp at the party. It's the only thing unusual I had, and I haven't had shrimp in years." Other times, a person may have hives come and go for months, without any clue as to cause. This is called chronic hives, and the cause cannot always be found, even with a doctor's help. High doses of antihistamines are often required as treatment.

Atopic Dermatitis (Eczema)

"The itch that rashes." Eczema is an extremely itchy rash found in older children and adults, in the folds of the elbow, knee, and elsewhere. Often it is scratched so vigorously that it bleeds, becomes infected, or both. People with this condition often have very dry skin; the rash itself is so dry it's almost scaly. Antihistamines do not work as well on eczema as they do on hives. Treatment can be complicated.

Who Can Help?

The allergies we have just described might seem to be a bewildering array of diseases. But no one has to face them alone.

One simple source of help is your school or public library. You may wish to read about allergies before seeking the help of anyone else, but in doing so you will learn that there are many people who are ready, willing, and able to help.

For advice about using over-the-counter medications for hay fever or hives, a pharmacist is a good person to ask. Pharmacists should also be able to provide answers to questions you may have about your prescriptions and be able to instruct you on proper use of inhalers and adrenaline injectors.

Your doctor is your single best and most reliable source for help. A wide range of treatments are available for allergic illnesses. The number of such treatments is growing larger every year.

For serious allergic problems you may want to consult an allergist. An allergist is a physician specially trained in the care of persons with allergic diseases. An allergist can try to track down the cause of the allergy as well as treat your symptoms. He or she will also make sure that you know how to use your nose or lung inhalers properly, making sure they work as effectively as possible. He or she is a great resource for you to consult.

Sinuses and Nasal Polyps

Our sinuses are cavities, or spaces, in the bones of the skull. They are all paired, left and right, and they surround the airways in our noses. They all drain into the sides of our noses. The maxillaries are the biggest, followed by the frontal sinuses. Though they are not present at birth, the frontal sinuses form fully by the teenage years.

No one knows for sure why we have sinuses. They may insulate our brains from cold air when we breathe. Hollow bones are lighter, so they make our heads weigh less. They also add resonance to our voices. The mucus they produce may help keep our noses moist.

A Flaw in the Design

The crucial fact about our sinuses can be summarized like this: Anatomy is destiny. Some sinuses—like the maxillary sinuses, located roughly below the cheekbones—drain upward. (By the way, this is a demonstration of evolution at work. Most mammals, such as dogs and cats, walk on four legs, with their heads hung down. In this position, sinuses drain downward. Have you ever heard of a dog with a sinus infection?) If you designed a sink, you would not put the drain high up on one side. Nonetheless, that's where our sinuses are. They work as well as they do

26

because the membranes lining our sinuses have tiny, fingerlike projections called cilia. (You may remember this term from biology class.) The cilia sweep the mucus produced by the membranes up to the openings in the nose, which are called the nostrils.

The same cilia are present in our nasal cavities. They sweep mucus and inhaled dirt back to our throat, where we swallow it. This keeps us from having an endlessly runny nose.

This backward flow of mucus explains why you cannot blow all the mucus out of your nose. At some point, your mother may have asked you not to sniffle or snort, but to "blow your nose!" Then you tried and found that you couldn't. The structure of your nasal bones and the function of the cilia on your nasal membranes prevent drainage from the front and encourage drainage into the throat. Which is why sniffling and snorting come naturally to even little children. (Your mother *was* right about those sounds not being polite, however.)

A number of things can stop the nasal cilia from working properly. Tobacco smoke and the viruses that cause the common cold are two common examples. When ciliary motion fails, our noses do not drain normally: they get runny up front and feel congested with the mucus that should be moving back and down. And the sinuses? The sinus cavities with upward drainage stop draining, so fluid pools at the bottom. Many people with colds will say that their faces feel "full." This is probably from fluid in their sinuses. Fluid pooled in our sinuses causes other problems, too. Have you ever seen the water that sits at the bottom of a clogged sink? It never looks good, and it is not something that you would want to drink. Likewise, the fluid that sits at the bottom of diseased sinuses tends to grow bacteria. This leads to sinus infections.

Sinus Infections

Another problem with the anatomy of our sinuses is that the openings are very small. They range, in adults, from two to six millimeters in width. They are even smaller in children. When the membranes in our noses get swollen, those openings may swell shut. This traps air, fluid, or both in the sinuses. The fluid is prone to infection. The lack of drainage makes these same infections hard to clear, even with antibiotics. The infected material simply has nowhere to drain.

Poor drainage also explains why sinus infections may last for months. The infected stuff is trapped. You may take antibiotics, which our bloodstream circulates into our tissues, but these must then leak out into the infected stuff to kill the bacteria. This is why chronic sinus infections (those that last longer than one month) often require long courses of antibiotics to clear. In many cases, twenty-one days of antibiotics are needed. Shorter courses just suppress the green drainage, which then comes back a few days after the antibiotics are done.

Such inadequate courses of antibiotics also promote bacterial resistance. So if you need antibiotics for a sinus infection, you need to take the whole prescription, not just enough until it seems better. And do not do what some people do—save some antibiotics for later on, "just in case." You will not have enough left to treat anything adequately. In case of problems later on, call your doctor. That's what he or she is there for.

If it seems as if everyone you know gets sinus infections, you may be right. Chronic sinusitis is a very common disease. It is more common than hay fever, arthritis, or high blood pressure. In any given year, it affects 15 percent of the population of the United States. Of all diseases, it is the fifth-leading cause of antibiotic use.

Not every cold (viral infection) causes a sinus (bacterial) infection. One study using CAT scans (a detailed type of X ray) found that 87 percent of patients with colds had accompanying sinus problems. Many people with colds blow out yellow-green mucus from their noses for a few days. After seven to ten days, the drainage should clear up, if not dry up. The "sinus" sensations (fullness, pressure, pain) should be going away by that point, and the excessive postnasal drip should be easing. If these symptoms continue, a true sinus infection could be involved.

Sinus Headaches

Sinuses cause other problems, too. Some people find that they get sinus headaches when the weather changes. Sinus anatomy explains how these occur. Barometric pressure changes as the weather changes, but the air trapped in closed sinuses has nowhere to go. Although the bony walls of the sinuses cannot move with pressure, they are sensitive to it. The result of this air trapped under pressure is sinus pain. In fact, people usually describe sinus headaches as feeling like "pressure."

The most common area where people feel sinus

headaches is between the eyebrows. This area is right over the ethmoidal sinuses. And it turns out that these are the sinuses that are most commonly diseased. They are small, and their small openings seem to get clogged easily.

Involvement of the frontal sinuses (above the eyes) and the maxillary sinuses (beneath the cheeks) seems to explain the sinus pain many people feel around their eyes. Have you known anyone whose teeth hurt when he or she had a sinus infection? The teeth in the upper jaw grow right into the floors and wall of the maxillary sinuses. The nerves that go into the teeth can run right under the sinus membrane lining, which leads to toothache when those membranes are inflamed from infection.

The Bones in the Nose

The bony wall that divides the inside of the nose into two nasal cavities is called the nasal septum (Latin for "wall"). It is never perfectly straight—there are no plumb lines in the womb. But most people have about the same amount of nasal air space on each side. If the septum really bows to one side, it can come up against the three bones—the turbinates—that come out of the side wall of the nose.

The specific details of the anatomy are not important here. What is important is that under the turbinates, many things drain through those little openings we discussed previously. The septum can push the turbinates back against the side wall of the nose and really narrow those openings. This can lead to repeated and chronic sinus infections on that side.

The side with the septum bowed into it will also feel

congested because not much air can move through it. If the membranes on the narrow side swell, that side may close completely off. Not to have air moving through one side of one's nose does not feel right. If a turbinate and the septum touch, this can cause a headache on that same side of the head. As you might expect, an ear, nose, and throat surgeon (an otorhinolaryngologist) can sometimes be of help in such situations.

You may hear of someone with a perforated septum, which has nothing to do with a nose ring. The nasal septum receives a very good supply of blood—a nose bleed comes from damage to one of the blood vessels on the surface of the septum. These same vessels, however, are exposed to things we inhale. Some drugs and medications can make the blood vessels close. If they close frequently, the septum loses its blood supply and part of it dies. And then there's a hole in the wall. Ear, nose, and throat surgeons can put a "button" in to stop whistling sounds and discomfort felt as air moves from one side to the other.

Snorting cocaine is a classic cause of a perforated septum. Overuse of nasal spray decongestants is another.

Nasal Polyps

If you do not know what nasal polyps are, you probably do not have them. A polyp is a growth or swelling of a membrane. Nasal polyps are smooth, pale blue, pear-shaped, and connected by a short stalk to their point of origin. They grow mostly out of the membranes that line the entrances to the sinuses. Although they are not cancerous growths, they are not normal tissues either. Polyps

31

have a texture like that of mucus because they are mostly water, held together by some cells and protein. They have no nerves, so they cannot "feel" anything.

If polyps are inside the nasal cavities, they can often be seen when a doctor examines the nose. They can also occur inside a sinus cavity, where they can be detected if sinus X rays are taken. A person with polyps in the nasal cavity may lose his or her sense of smell because air cannot get to the upper part of the nose, which is where the smell sensors are located. Polyps may fill one nasal passage so completely that no air moves on that side. On occasion they get so large that they push out on the nasal bones and cause nasal deformities.

Although doctors really do not know how common nasal polyps are, they do know other things about them. They typically occur in people over forty years of age. They are twice as common in men. Polyps are rarely seen in the noses of children younger than ten, with the important exception of children with a very serious disease called cystic fibrosis (CF). Polyps in the nose of a child younger than ten are often an indicator of CF.

Doctors used to think that finding polyps in someone's nose meant that the person had allergies, but we now know that is not necessarily true. Nasal polyps are not more common in allergic people. One study that examined 3,000 allergic patients found that only one-half of 1 percent had nasal polyps.

How nasal polyps form and exactly what causes them is still unclear. One common thread is the presence of sinus disease. The sinus problems can be associated with allergy or infection or bone-structure problems—it does not seem to matter. This may be why most polyps grow from the sinus entrances.

Nasal Polyps and Asthma

There is definitely a connection between nasal polyps and asthma. In one large study of 5,000 patients with hay fever or asthma, 211 people (4 percent of the whole group) had polyps. Seventy percent of those with polyps had asthma. Of the total number of people with asthma, 17 percent had nasal polyps. But of those patients with hay fever, only 2 percent had polyps. In another study, 20 percent of patients with nasal polyps also had asthma.

How are polyps and asthma linked? Scientists have established two connections: sinus infections, which predispose people both to polyps and to asthma; and something called "aspirin-sensitive asthma," where patients develop a runny, stuffy nose not caused by allergies, and then they get nasal polyps. Later asthma develops. Later still, they find that if they take anti-inflammatory pain relievers such as aspirin, ibuprofen, or naproxen (but not acetaminophen), they experience a flare-up of their asthma and nasal disease. Studies of nasal polyp patients have shown that 8 percent have some degree of "aspirin sensitivity."

Sinusitis and Asthma

Physicians believe that sinus infections often trigger or worsen asthma. Although this observation was first made in 1925, it has been difficult to prove, primarily because people with hay fever often have both sinus problems and asthma and it is often difficult to establish which came first. Scientists do have some evidence, though. For example, children whose sinus X-ray results are abnormal are three times more likely to be admitted to a hospital for asthma. In another study, 87 percent of adults with asthma flare-ups had abnormal sinus X-rays.

No one knows how this works or why it should be true. Very little infected postnasal drip can get to the lungs, because our voice box (larynx) keeps it out. There appears to be a reflex connection between the upper and lower airways (the nose and the lungs). Disease upstream makes for trouble downstream.

What happens once the sinus disease is treated? The asthma quiets down. In one study of children with sinus infections and asthma, 70 percent needed fewer asthma medications and 67 percent had normal lung-function tests once the sinusitis was treated. Another study tracked adults who had undergone surgery to open their sinuses. Sixty percent had reduced need for asthma medications over the following five years.

Allergies That Affect Your Breathing

The nose and the lungs are different organs, but they respond somewhat similarly when affected by allergy. Before we get into the details, let's take a very brief spin into the airways for some anatomy terms.

Inhaled air comes into the nose and goes through the nasal passages to the throat. Air then goes down through the voice box, or larynx, into the chest in the bronchial passages, or bronchi. The bronchi bring air into the lung tissue, where oxygen is absorbed and carbon dioxide is released. Exhaled air goes out in the reverse order.

This is also a good time to mention some technical terms. Asthma is a disease of inflamed bronchial passages. In general, inflammation of the bronchi is called bronchitis, although that term is more properly reserved for bacterial infections of the bronchi. Some people with bronchitis wheeze until they get over the infection. A good way to think of asthma is as allergic bronchitis, although it is not called that.

If bronchitis is inflamed bronchial passages, then rhinitis must be . . . inflamed nasal passages. (The term is derived from the Greek word *rhis*, which means "nose." The same derivation also gives rise to words such as rhinoplasty, which is the medical term for the surgical procedure commonly referred to as a nose job, and also to rhinoceros.) The most common kind of rhinitis is viral (caused by a virus)—the common cold. The medical term for hay fever is allergic rhinitis. One reason why a cold can feel so much like hay fever, and vice versa, is because both are kinds of rhinitis.

Hay Fever (Allergic Rhinitis)

Hay fever is the most common allergic disease. By some estimates, 10 to 20 percent of the U.S. population is afflicted with hay fever to some degree. However, each person's symptoms can vary greatly—just ask any two people with hay fever.

If you stop to think about how a person with hay fever is typically portrayed in television commercials, many of the classic symptoms will immediately come to mind. The nose is stuffy, red, and may even look a bit swollen, especially if it has been blown a lot. It drips up front, and what comes out is clear and runny. A lot of fluid drains down the back of the nose into the throat under normal circumstances, but now there is a waterfall. This leads to a feeling of mucus in the back of the throat (what doctors call postnasal drip). Often, the person needs to clear his throat and cough frequently. The throat can become itchy, as can the nose. Even the insides of the ears can feel itchy.

Eye symptoms are common. Sometimes they bother people more than the nasal symptoms. Eyelids can swell. The whites of the eyes get red because lots of small blood vessels open up. The white part of the eye may even swell a bit. Itching is very common, and rubbing only makes the itching worse. The eyes water, which only makes the runny nose that much worse.

When the nasal linings swell, the nose does not work properly. This is true no matter what causes the swelling—virus or allergies. The sinus entrances can swell shut, which traps air, fluid, or both in the sinuses and can cause sinus headaches. The nasal passages then have much less room for air to pass through them. This makes it much harder to breathe through your nose. Even giving your nose a nice, hard, honking blow is not enough to clear the swollen membranes. It merely irritates them, which makes things worse. (It may also make your ears pop, from air forced into the eustachian tubes.) So you end up breathing through your mouth in order to get enough air.

Mucus, like any liquid, can pool. Many people find that if they have hay fever and lie on their backs, they cough persistently. This is from mucus pooling in the back of their throats. So they often lie on their sides, breathing through the mouth. Being on your side helps to keep you from drooling on the pillow.

This does not sound like a comfortable way to sleep, and it is not. Breathing through your mouth also promotes snoring, which is the sound made by the back part of the roof of the mouth (the soft palate) as it flutters with breath inhaled through the nose and the mouth simultaneously. Snoring is worse when the snorer is lying flat on his back. Many people with bad hay fever (and bad colds) snore because they are trying to breathe normally—through their noses—and they cannot. While most adult snorers are heavyset men, anyone with hay fever might snore.

Many children with hay fever (and colds) also snore. Their noses have smaller air passages than the noses of grown-ups do. They often also have big adenoids, which are like lymph glands at the top of the throat. They can grow to be very large. If they do, the soft palate can flutter against them, and, oh boy, can the snoring get loud.

The way that hay fever (and other allergies) can impair sleep contributes greatly to what doctors call allergic fatigue. People with hay fever often feel exhausted, morning till night. Although doctors still do not know all the reasons for this, it probably has a lot to do with the inability to get a good night's sleep. Studies have shown that people with ongoing hay fever feel worse than people with ongoing asthma, so it is not just the difficulty of breathing that causes the fatigue.

Hay fever (or its seasonal counterpart, rose fever) originally earned its name because people became so ill from it that they felt as if they were running a fever. Of course, doctors now know they did not really have fevers. But imagine how bad hay fever must have felt for someone who lived and worked on a farm 100 or more years ago, before science had developed very effective treatments. Some people were virtually disabled from the disease.

Of course, for many people, hay fever does not always have such severe effects, then or now. What's more, one member of a family can display no symptoms at all, another might have allergies so mild as to rarely even require over-the-counter medications, while another experiences bothersome symptoms year-round.

Hay fever usually starts in childhood. Sufferers tend to have their symptoms improve after age forty. Nevertheless, people of every age come down with hay fever, seemingly from out of the blue. A common question that allergists hear is "Why did I get this now?"

Sometimes, there is no easy answer, although some clues are usually available. The patient may have had persistent exposure to a cat or a dog for the first time. Or he or she may be living in a temperate climate for the first time. Hay fever is more common in temperate than tropical climates, perhaps because of greater amounts of pollen grains and mold spores in the air in certain seasons.

Doctors tend to label rhinitis by whether it is seasonal or year-round—seasonal or perennial rhinitis. This is significant because someone with purely seasonal rhinitis is typically ill for only one or two of the four seasons. Rather than go to the doctor, people with seasonal symptoms often try to muddle through or use over-the-counter remedies. With no seasonal break in their suffering, people with perennial symptoms more often turn to their doctors for help. Many of the patients that we see as physicians have a background of perennial symptoms that grow even worse in certain seasons.

Spring and fall have the worst reputations for causing hay fever, but for many people in colder climates, winter is the worst. Windows stay closed. Heating systems recirculate the same old air. Modern houses tend to be well insulated and snug, which means that little fresh air leaks in from the outside. Indoor heating season is also virus season. There is no one single reason for why this is so, but people being together indoors seems to be part of the explanation. Winter is a bad season for many people, allergic or not, because it is virus season, and colds can lead to sinus infections. In the winter, people stay crowded together with their indoor allergens (such as pets) and their viruses (such as colds). This makes winter sinus season for many people, too.

Which brings up another point: Not everyone with rhinitis is allergic. You can have the stuffy nose and post-nasal drip of hay fever but not have allergic rhinitis. What can cause rhinitis besides allergies (and viruses)?

One problem can be what is called structural rhinitis. The nasal septum can have bony spurs that stick out from each side, or it can be badly deviated. The bones on the side of the nose can overgrow the space available to them. Or a combination of these can happen, with the end result that the air has little space to move through. The membranes lining these narrow air channels then seem to become easily irritated and inflamed.

Asthma

What, exactly, is asthma?

This question has proved very hard to answer. To people with asthma, the illness usually has at least some of the following features: reversible shortness of breath, a sensation of tightness in the chest, wheezing sounds, cough (which sometimes brings up mucus), sleep distur-bance, and problems with exercise and cold air.

Asthma is growing more common, not only in the United States but around the world. About 5 percent of the people in the United States have asthma. Approximately 5,000 people in the United States still die of asthma every year, despite the many advances that have been made in its diagnosis and treatment.

Many people have both hay fever and asthma. For the majority of hay fever sufferers under the age of fifty, this is true. For most of them, the hay fever came first.

For many years, asthmatics were portrayed in the media as people afraid of the world because they had been disabled by their illness—children who could not come out to play, adults who were weaklings. This perception has changed somewhat in recent years, perhaps because there have been several prominent Olympic athletes with asthma. The perception should soon change even more because there are now a variety of effective and convenient treatments for asthma, for young and old sufferers alike.

Asthma differs for each person who has it. Some people experience symptoms only occasionally. These people might use only a symptom-relieving inhaler, as needed. Asthma with this pattern of symptoms is called intermittent asthma. People with this degree of asthma rarely have nighttime symptoms or severe shortness of breath.

Related to this category of asthma are problems doctors call cold-induced asthma and exercise-induced asthma. Cold air, from winter temperatures or commercial refrigeration units, is the culprit in the first instance. The latter problem occurs with or a few minutes after exertion strong enough to make one breathe hard and fast. In fact, hyperventilating without exertion—simple overbreathing—can often make someone with asthma wheeze.

This reaction of asthmatic airways to cold air or fast air movement is another characteristic feature of asthma. In many cases, the airways of asthmatics are abnormally twitchy. Any mild irritation seems to set them off. Not everyone with asthma experiences this, but many do.

Doctors may use this feature of asthma to help diagnose it through what are called provocation tests. Such tests may be used when someone might have asthma but the doctor is not absolutely sure. The patient inhales chemicals, in doses too low to irritate normal lungs, that make the airways spasm. In this way, doctors can see how irritable the patient's airways are.

Physicians call asthma persistent when its symptoms are present daily. Whether it is judged to be mild or severe depends on how bad the symptoms are each day. People with persistent asthma need to use medication regularly to keep their asthma under control.

The presence or absence of night symptoms are an important gauge of asthma's severity in a patient. Persistent asthma almost always displays nocturnal symptoms, although, like other symptoms of asthma, these are not the same for everyone. The timing certainly varies from person to person. The symptoms can occur after suppertime, at bedtime, overnight, or first thing in the morning. Overnight is the worst time for many people with asthma; they wake up in the small hours of the morning, wheezing, coughing, and short of breath. In general, more frequent and more severe night symptoms mean that the asthma will be more difficult to control.

Finally, there is the unfortunate asthma sufferer who wheezes all the time. His or her life is controlled by asthma. He or she may try to control the asthma through behavior, thinking things such as "If I don't move fast, and I sit still, I won't be short of breath." The person may try to get by with over-the-counter remedies from the pharmacy instead of getting prescriptions renewed. This can be very dangerous. Such severe asthma threatens a person's life, and he or she needs to get treatment. With modern treatment methods, very few people with asthma need to experience constant symptoms.

The Asthmatic Lung: An Inside View

So what exactly is going on inside the lungs of a person with asthma?

Doctors know a good deal about this. When someone has an asthma attack, the muscles around the airways spasm. This reduces the size of the breathing passages. At the same time, the membranes lining the breathing passages produce mucus. This clogs the breathing passages. The membranes themselves swell, too. The combined result is small airways that do not move the normal amount of air. If the muscles spasm greatly and more mucus is produced than can be coughed up, a person with asthma loses the ability to get enough air. The result is increased difficulty breathing and, in severe enough cases, death.

The cause of the inflammation is often but not always allergic. Viruses, especially cold viruses and influenza (the flu), trigger wheezing in people with asthma. Influenza, in particular, can cause many weeks of wheezing. (So it is much better to get the yearly immunization.) For some people with asthma, rhinitis, or both, doctors are never able to find exactly what has caused their airways to be inflamed. But the inflammation is real, nevertheless, and physicians treat it aggressively.

You may know someone, perhaps a parent or older relative, who suffers from the disease known as emphysema, which also causes wheezing, coughing, and difficulty in breathing. But asthma differs from emphysema in one extremely important way: reversibility. One of the most important features of asthma is the fact that the inflamed

43

airways can be opened and soothed with treatment, so that lung function comes back to normal.

In contrast, emphysema is damage and destruction of the lung tissue, usually due to decades spent inhaling hot, dry tobacco smoke. When the lung tissue itself is damaged, it heals with scarring. This scarring distorts the nearby small airways. No amount of treatment can reverse this scarring.

A related ailment is chronic bronchitis, which is characterized by damaged, chronically infected airways. Patients with this illness may wheeze and cough up mucus, as people with asthma do. The main differences are that in the person with chronic bronchitis, the mucus is often infected and not allergic and that no amount of treatment will bring the airways back to health. The goal of the doctor treating a patient with chronic bronchitis is to make the airways as well as possible. Doctors often group emphysema and chronic bronchitis together as chronic obstructive lung disease because most people with one of these ailments also have the other.

Can infants have asthma? By definition, no, because asthma cannot officially be diagnosed in someone younger than two. For sure, there are "wheezy babies." Babies have small airways that can whistle for a number of reasons: viral infections such as colds; inhaling small items; cystic fibrosis; food allergy reactions; and other reasons. Baby boys wheeze more often, too. But a diagnosis of asthma requires that the lungs and immune system reach a level of development that is usually seen around a child's second birthday.

Like, but Not Exactly Alike

Two terms are often used for asthmalike symptoms. The first is "asthmatic bronchitis," which you or someone you know may have been diagnosed with. As you learned earlier in this chapter, asthma really is a sort of bronchitis. Many physicians use the term asthmatic bronchitis for episodes of wheezing associated with a chest infection of some sort.

The other term is "reactive airways disease." This term is sometimes used for persistent wheezing in children under two years of age, who cannot properly be diagnosed with asthma. It may also be used when someone of any age develops wheezing, coughing, and shortness of breath after inhaling large amounts of irritating industrial smoke, fumes, or gases. It may also be used by physicians when a patient has symptoms of asthma but the physician does not feel comfortable using the term asthma.

You may hear other terms, such as "asthmatoid bronchitis" and "wheezy baby." One major problem with all these terms is that for some patients they might more properly be called asthma. The use of these terms can prevent someone who really has asthma from receiving proper treatment.

Asthma and Reflux (Heartburn)

Over the past couple of decades, doctors have learned that in many people, food comes back up the food pipe. The food pipe is called the esophagus, and the process of food leaking back up it is called esophageal reflux, or "reflux" for short. This often causes what people experience as heartburn, but often it does not hurt at all or cause any other symptoms.

Doctors do not know why some people have a leaky valve at the top of their stomachs. Nor do we know why some people experience no discomfort or other sensation when reflux takes place. Reflux most often occurs after meals, when the stomach is full. Straining, bending over, and lying down soon after meals (going to bed with a full stomach) all tend to make stomach contents go back up the esophagus. Some foods, such as onions, mint, and chocolate, and some medications also promote reflux. Despite what many people believe, "spicy" foods do not promote reflux in someone unless the person has it anyway.

Physicians have also learned that asthma and reflux very frequently occur together. In some studies, more than 50 percent of people with reflux—sometimes as high as 65 percent—also have asthma. This includes children, who rarely experience heartburn.

Asthma can be triggered or worsened by reflux. The mechanism appears to be a reflex (no, not the reflux reflex) that triggers airway spasms when food or acid enters the esophagus from the stomach. Perhaps this reflex reaction evolved to keep food from being inhaled in case of vomiting. Whatever the reason, it can make asthma much worse.

Doctors tend to suspect reflux in asthma patients (without heartburn) in two settings. The first is patients with asthma that proves hard to control even with the use of appropriate medications and proper attention to allergy issues. The second is wheezing and coughing that comes on after bedtime, that is, after the patients lie down flat. In children in particular, nighttime worsening of asthma symptoms should lead a doctor to suspect reflux.

Doctors use various tests to pinpoint reflux activity. The

important point is that someone thinks of reflux as a possible cause, even in children without heartburn. There are now medications that dramatically improve reflux control. When reflux is well controlled, the associated asthma usually shows improvement as well. Because in most cases reflux can be controlled but not cured, treatment needs to be ongoing.

Upstream, Downstream

Two ailments have been proven to make asthma worse. One is esophageal reflux. The other is . . . hay fever.

Doctors learned this by conducting studies of the treatment of hay fever with nasal steroids. These proved to be very effective treatments for hay fever, but associated asthma also got better. The effect was greater with nasal steroids than with weaker treatments. A couple of the newer, less sedating antihistamines also improve asthma a bit. This may also be one mechanism by which allergy shots work.

The reason this works appears to be the same nose-lung reflex you read about in Chapter 2. This reflex seems to operate for both sinus infections and hay fever. So if you have asthma and hay fever, they both need treatment.

You're Allergic to What?

Not just anything that floats in the air can be an allergen. In fact, airborne particles must have specific characteristics in order to be real allergens. With the important exception of dust mite allergens, an inhaled allergen is characterized by:

⮑ Wide distribution of source—the plant (or mold or animal) must be common, so that it puts out allergens in lots of places.

⮑ Abundant production—by all sources.

⮑ Being windborne—so that it can be carried to the nose.

⮑ Being the right size to be inhaled—specifically, this means particles 15 to 50 microns in diameter. (A micron or micrometer is one-one thousandth of a millimeter.)

⮑ Allergenic potency—the ingredients of the particle must trigger the immune system to make an allergic response.

These principles explain why people are very rarely allergic to flowering plants. Flowers are plant technology, designed by nature to get insects and birds to come to the plant and carry and spread its pollen around. This means that pollen does not float around in the air—animals carry it from place to place. And if it is not in the air, you cannot inhale it. This is why the old term for spring allergy symptoms, rose fever, is a misnomer—there is no airborne rose pollen. (Grass blooms at the same time.) The same is true for people who say, "I'm allergic to cottonwood," a tree that blooms in grass season, and "I have goldenrod hay fever," which is usually hay fever that is actually caused by the pollinating ragweed growing right next to the goldenrod.

Wind-pollinated plants must produce large numbers of

pollen if any of the pollen is to have a decent chance of reaching another plant. What this means is that it needs to fill the nearby air with pollen. The pollen also needs to be small and light so that it can travel to plants that may be far away—or to our noses. The pollen does not come from "flowers" but from "inflorescences" or groups of flowers.

Outdoor Allergens

Outdoor allergens fall into two categories: pollen grains and mold spores. The National Allergy Bureau, an association of allergists, records and organizes pollen and mold spore counts for the United States. The following discussion, derived in part from its work, applies to nondesert areas of the United States.

We often feel that the air is "cleaner" after a rainstorm. Two factors are at work here. The first is that rain washes particles out of the air, and the longer the rain, the more is washed out of the air. Second, lightning produces a different form of oxygen, ozone, in the air. The ozone molecule is very reactive and breaks up other chemicals in the air. This is something like bleaching the air. (Ozone is also a factor in air pollution. Too much in the air damages our airways and makes asthma flare.)

Pollen

Pollen is almost constantly present in outdoor air in warm weather. This appears to be one reason why allergic rhinitis (hay fever) is more common here than in the tropics. Tropical plants primarily use flowers and insects to move pollen. In a temperate region, plants start to bloom at the start of the spring thaw.

The first type of pollen to come in the spring is from trees. Trees bloom in the early spring, which starts in January farthest south: Georgia, Florida, Louisiana, Texas, Oklahoma, and California. The bloom moves north as the months pass. In most states, the bloom begins in February and March. Only in New Hampshire, Vermont, Wisconsin, Minnesota, Montana, and North Dakota do the trees bloom as late as April. In Alaska, the bloom begins in May!

The most important trees for allergy sufferers are the ones known as deciduous, which shed their leaves each autumn. Examples of deciduous trees are oaks, maples, and birches. Each spring, such trees put out pollen anthers, an inch or two in length, from all available twigs. The tree becomes, in effect, a giant pollen factory. Depending on various weather conditions, especially moisture, tree pollen season lasts two to three months.

In some areas—Oklahoma, Texas, and the Pacific Northwest—cedar trees are known to be important sources of allergens. Research is underway in other areas. Though cedars are coniferous, or evergreen, trees, other conifers are not a cause of allergic symptoms, even though they are wind-pollinated. Why? Two reasons. First, their pollen is very heavy and falls to the ground rapidly. Second, they just do not seem to be allergenic (capable of causing allergies).

After tree pollen comes pollen from grasses. Grass pollen comes from small, almost feathery structures that appear at the end of stalks. The stalks themselves can be very short, so grass pollen can come from grass of every height, even from neatly mowed lawns. In the South in the United States, the grass pollen season starts in March; in the North it begins in May. The kinds of grass vary from south to north, but all can cause allergies. Grass season also lasts two to three months.

Weeds are the next source of pollen. Weeds may be defined as broad-leaved annuals that grow in disturbed soil, pavement cracks, and other marginal and wayside areas. Because weeds are not cultivated but tend to grow spread-out over a large geographical area, they rely on wind pollination.

Ragweed is the prototype. Before AD 1500, this weed was found on scattered river beds. In order for its pollen to reach other ragweeds and reproduce, the ragweed plant evolved to produce as much as one billion pollen grains per plant. Ragweed spreads aggressively and can now be found in almost every state. According to recent pollen counts, the three exceptions are Idaho, Oregon, and Alaska.

Some weeds come out in the middle of grass season: plantain (check a nearby lawn) and sheep sorrel, for example. These also fade away during the summer. Weed season usually starts a month or two after grass season ebbs. This is why hay fever sufferers often feel better in the middle of the summer.

If we use ragweed and sage as markers, in southern areas of the United States autumn weeds begin to put out pollen at the end of July, gradually increasing production until they reach full force in mid-August. How can a weed be so specific about the time when it produces pollen? As fall approaches, production is triggered by the shortening length of the day. Stressful conditions, such as drought, make the plants "bloom" early.

Weed season lasts until the weeds cannot survive any longer. In northern areas, this means until the first hard frost.

Molds

There are mold spores in the outdoor air whenever the ground is not covered with snow, which makes most of the year mold season. Molds, which are also known as fungi, are found in soil everywhere and are what give it that "earthy" smell. Edible mushrooms, appropriately, have the same sort of smell.

There are thousands of species of mold. The role of molds in nature is mostly to help break up and decompose dead things—plants and animals. So they tend to be found more in areas of rotting debris of any sort, including piles of leaves. Autumn is sometimes called mold season because mold spores increase as the pollen count from weeds decreases.

Spores are the tiny airborne structures by which molds are spread. Technically, they are not seeds, but the idea is the same. They are released into the air by the millions. If they land somewhere moist, they can germinate and seek nutrition. This is one very good reason why molds are so very common: To get started, all they need is a little bit of moisture. Even in the deserts of Arizona and New Mexico, mold spores are present year-round.

Indoor Allergens

Indoor allergens are always present, but their effects become more noticeable in the winter, when people tend to be inside more. The heat is turned on and the windows are closed, so the indoor air is recirculated, complete with allergens and viruses. American houses built since the energy crisis of 1973–74 tend to have excellent insulation. They also are well sealed to keep out drafts—which also keeps out fresh air. Poor air circulation also means that indoor allergens are not moved out as quickly as they would be in the spring, for example, when windows are more likely to be left open.

Molds

Since molds can be found outdoors anywhere there is a bit of moisture and warmth, it is no surprise that they are found all over the great indoors, too. Some mold is found in the earth around houseplants, but basements are usually the worst offenders. By definition, basements are holes in the ground. As such, they naturally tend to be cool and dark and moist—ideal conditions for fungus. For a variety of reasons, many basements flood intermittently. Others collect standing water. Dirt floors tend to be constantly damp. Concrete floors also hold moisture. Once soaked, carpet on a concrete basement floor never dries completely. So mold grows luxuriantly on old basement carpeting. If the basement walls are old and discolored, some of that discoloration is probably also from mildew.

Other sources of mold are the other sources of water in the house. Showers make nice, wet surfaces for mildew, as do shower curtains and bathtubs. Water can sometimes be found standing around kitchen faucets— mold can grow there, too.

Pets

If you have allergic problems, it is probably not a wise idea to get a furred or feathered pet. Any allergic person is at risk of developing allergic sensitivity to such pets. Most mammal and bird pets are sources of potent allergens, and sensitivity often develops after a year or two.

Cats

Cats make a few minor allergens and one major allergen. That major allergen comes from the skin and saliva in vast, stupendous quantity. The old chestnut, "I have a short-haired cat so it can't bother me," is a comforting self-deception. Some cats do seem to put out less allergens than others, but this cannot be predicted on the basis of coat or breed or any known factor.

Because cats put out a tremendous amount of allergens, if you have a cat somewhere, you have a cat everywhere. Cat allergen floats easily in the air but is also very sticky. If you have a cat, the allergen is stuck to your clothes, the carpeting, the bedding, and your hands if you pet the cat. Cat allergen has been found at the top of the Empire State Building, a very windy place where no cats go. It is often found in the offices of allergists, where people bring it on their clothes. Keeping the cat out of your bedroom does not help allergies; washing the cat weekly does nothing; restricting the cat to one room does no good.

Other Pets

Dogs put out less allergen, and less potent allergen, than cats. That said, they still cause people allergic problems. With guinea pigs, hamsters, mice, rabbits, and rats, the allergen comes mostly from the urine (as it evaporates). Birds also excrete allergen, partly from their feathers.

House Dust Mites

House dust mites are tiny, sightless, eight-legged creatures that live by eating our dander. (Not a pretty thought, but true.) They have been found everywhere people use cloth—even on the space shuttle! They are invisible to the naked eye: When fully grown and well fed, they are at most 0.3 millimeters long (one millimeter being about 1/16 of an inch). They live in cloth; they hang on to and crawl around on the fibers. They take their name from the easiest place to find them.

Their usual habitat, though, is carpeting, clothing, upholstery, and bedding. They need to live in warm (65 to 80 degrees Fahrenheit) and moist (50 percent or greater humidity) places. Cloth holds moisture. The mites have no source of water except the air, so they need to stay in humid environments. Even when the air is dry, the air between the cloth fibers in our bedding is moist from our overnight perspiration. All the cloth surfaces in bedding provide lots of surface area to hold moisture. To a lesser degree, upholstery and carpeting can do the same thing. But the bedding is the important part because it is in the bedding that we come into contact with dust mite allergen.

People are not allergic to the actual dust mites themselves but to their waste matter: components in their fecal pellets (not a pretty thought.) The important word here is pellets. They are bigger (50 to 60 microns) and heavier than pollen grains or mold spores. They do not float in the air. If you fluff bedding, within thirty minutes later all of the dust mite allergen has settled back into it. To be exposed to the allergen you have to roll around on cloth surfaces. We all are exposed when we roll around in our bedding—that is, every night. Small children also get exposed when they crawl and roll around on rugs and carpets.

People not only inhale dust mite pellets but also have their skin come in contact with them. For some people, particularly adults, this seems to be an important cause of atopic dermatitis.

Cockroaches

These six-legged insects are pests in cities throughout North America. They are associated with filth, but once they have colonized a large building it is almost impossible to exterminate them if they have a water supply—such as a toilet. They can eat almost anything, but they thrive on human garbage. They usually are found in tremendous numbers in any building they inhabit. In the South, where they survive out-of-doors due to the mild winters, they are sometimes called "palmetto bugs." Outdoor survival makes it easier for them to invade homes.

When cockroaches die, their bodies dry out and break apart. They then become an ingredient of the house's dust, to be inhaled.

Plain Old House Dust

You have probably heard people complain that they are allergic to dust and that it makes them sneeze. Allergists used to test people for house dust. Then, as scientists learned about mold spores and pet dander and dust mites and cockroaches, a new question arose: Exactly what is house dust?

The answer: nothing in particular. House dust is just a collection of small bits of stuff. Dust may contain fibers of cloth, hairs, dander from people and pets, pollen grains, mold spores, dust mites, insect parts, food bits, and almost anything else imaginable. Your house dust is unique; someone else's will not be exactly the same and you will not respond to it in quite the same way. So you cannot be allergic to house dust in the same way that you can to a pure allergen such as ragweed pollen. But it is no wonder that it might make you sneeze or wheeze and that some dust will make you sneeze more than other dust will.

Food Allergies, Hay Fever, and Asthma

Many people wonder if food allergies are the cause of their breathing problems. Popular magazines often feature articles about "hidden food allergies." But in fact, the bulk of scientific evidence now points to a simple answer.

Mild food allergies are related to skin diseases such as hives and atopic dermatitis. More severe allergic reactions to food are a form of anaphylaxis—whole body allergic reactions. These usually feature hives and swelling of the lip, tongue, and throat; nausea, vomiting, and diarrhea; runny nose, wheezing, and shortness of breath; and sometimes even low blood pressure, with fainting and even death.

If you think about it, it does not make sense that the immune system would give a person only breathing symptoms when the source of the symptoms is in the stomach and bowels. Likewise, inhaled allergens do not cause hives. They cause rhinitis and asthma—that is, the symptoms appear where the allergens contact the immune system.

Some people notice that their nose gets runny or stuffy or that they feel tight-chested and wheezy after drinking beer or especially wine. This is a reaction to those foods— from their inhaled vapors or from the alcohol.

For example, wine is preserved with sulfites. Sulfites evaporate easily and come off the wine with each sip. Sulfites are also an ingredient in air pollution. People without breathing problems rarely have problems with sulfites, but many allergic and asthmatic people have airways that react strongly to them. Beer has other compounds that bother allergic and asthmatic people.

The other factor is alcohol itself. It gives some people flushed cheeks. Others get swelling and flushing inside their noses. This then causes nasal congestion and a runny nose. The treatment for alcohol- and sulfite-related nasal or bronchial reactions is to avoid alcoholic beverages.

Many people find that when they eat "hot" foods, their noses run. This may be true for temperature-hot foods as well as spicy-hot ones. (For an experiment, the next time you are at a Chinese restaurant, have the hot and sour soup.) Heat (both kinds) in foods causes the blood vessels in your nose to open, just as it causes your mouth to salivate. But there is no rhinitis because your nose is not inflamed, just runny.

Irritants

Irritants are defined as inhaled substances that directly irritate our airways. Many things we inhale are irritants. Smoke, for one. Tobacco smoke is hot, dry, and full of chemicals derived from the burning tobacco leaf itself. It is no wonder that for many people, exposure to tobacco smoke causes their noses and lungs to become inflamed. Wood smoke is also an irritant, although daily exposure is uncommon outside of woodstove-heated houses. The sulfites discussed above are irritants. Many other air pollutants are irritants. Smog creates breathing difficulties for many people. Some people find that strong odors of all sorts—potpourri and perfumes, for example—make their noses and lungs act up.

Stinging Insects and Anaphylaxis

Killer bees! They attack all at once and seemingly without provocation. A swarm of killer bees will chase you for half a mile. If you jump in a swimming pool or pond, they hover around and wait for you to come up for air. These "killer bees" originated in Brazil after a beekeeper imported some African bees that mixed with the local bee population, in the process transmitting to their offspring five genes that have been linked to aggressive behavior and a tendency to sting.

The new breed of bees attacks twenty times faster and deposits eight times more stings in the first twenty seconds than do regular honeybees. Swarms of these critters, which now inhabit Latin America and some parts of the southwestern United States, have been responsible for the deaths of livestock and even some people.

Despite its suddenness and horror, death in these cases does not result from an allergic reaction. Instead, death comes from the massive number of stings and injection of toxic substances in the venom from many bees.

In contrast, if you are stung by a single honeybee or another stinging insect in the *Hymenoptera* order of insects (wasp, yellow jacket, hornet, fire ant) and you develop diffuse, itching hives all over your body, swelling of your eyes, ears, or lips, difficulty swallowing, tightness or swelling in your throat, tightness in your chest, wheezing, lightheadedness, or fainting, then you are having an acute, immediate, life-threatening allergic anaphylactic reaction. This happens because your immune system reacts to one or more of the allergenic proteins present in the small amount of insect venom injected into you by the sting.

So these, too, can be "killer bees." These insects are found throughout the world. And for certain individuals, perhaps even you, their stings can be lethal, accounting for 40 to 150 deaths in the United States each year. More than 500,000 people per year are treated in hospital emergency rooms in the United States for insect bites and stings.

The Whys of Anaphylaxis

The immune system of an allergic person may be prone to produce IgE antibodies to insect venom after the first sting. Most allergic people do not experience a severe allergic reaction at the time of a first sting. In fact, many people who have allergic sting reactions do not recall having been previously stung.

Nevertheless, after a second or third sting by another insect of the same or related species, the insect venom allergens combine with the IgE antibody that was previously produced in response to the earlier sting. The combination of venom allergen and IgE antibody triggers the release of histamine and other chemical mediators, which cause allergic symptoms. The severity of reactions can range from large local reactions to the immediate life-threatening allergic reactions known as anaphylaxis.

Signs and Symptoms of Anaphylaxis

Anaphylaxis is a medical emergency. Anaphylaxis develops rapidly, within minutes, after an insect sting or within sixty minutes after ingestion of a food allergen or drug allergen. Interestingly, it does not appear that if you are allergic to stings that you are more prone to become allergic to foods or drugs (medicines) or the reverse. Scientists still do not know for sure whether people who have other common allergic conditions, such as eczema, hay fever, or asthma, are more prone to develop allergy to stinging insects.

However, it is known that if you have asthma and are also allergic to stings, then you are apt to have a very severe reaction when stung. This observation holds true for asthma and food allergy and for asthma and drug allergy. In fact, it is also true for asthmatic patients who are receiving allergen vaccines (allergen immunotherapy injections).

The signs and symptoms of anaphylaxis include any one or a combination of the following:

↪ Flushing and itching of the entire body

↪ Hives all over the body

↪ Swelling of the throat or tongue

↪ Difficulty breathing

↪ Cough, wheezing, or chest tightness

↪ Dizziness

↪ Headache

↪ Stomach cramps, nausea, vomiting, or diarrhea

In severe cases of anaphylaxis, there may be a rapid fall in blood pressure and loss of consciousness, which is called anaphylactic shock. People who have survived this type of reaction have described experiencing a feeling of "impending doom." Pretty scary, to say the least. So if you have this problem, what do you need to know and what should you do about it?

Know Your Enemy

If you do not know which insects sting, where they hide, and when they sting, you will be relying just on luck to avoid being stung. Knowledge gives you the power to have control over your health and some degree of control over your destiny. Stinging insects are most active during the summer and early fall, when the populations of nests can exceed 60,000 insects. Life-threatening stings come from five types of insects: honeybees, paper wasps, yellow jackets, hornets, and fire ants. These are found throughout the United States, except for fire ants, which are found only in the southeastern states.

Honeybees are about one-half to one inch long and have a rounded, hairy, dark brown body with yellow markings. Domesticated honeybees live in man-made hives; wild honeybees make their honeycomb nests in the hollows of trees and cavities of buildings. They will sting only if provoked. Because their stinger is barbed, they frequently leave it and its attached venom sac on the victim.

Honeybees die after stinging because they are eviscerated as they are separated from their stingers and venom sacs when they fly or are swatted away. Because honeybees gather their nectar to make honey from white clover, a weed that grows on lawns throughout the United States, children frequently step on them while playing barefoot in the grass and get stung on the bottom of the foot or between the toes.

Yellow jackets are black with yellow markings and are about the same size as honeybees, but they do not have barbed stingers. Thus, a single yellow jacket can sting several times. Their nests are found under rotted wood, logs, and leaves in underground holes. They frequently hover around garbage cans that are stored outside and at picnic sites. Yellow jackets also like to investigate the inside of soda pop cans and bottles; stings on the lips, on the tongue, or in the throat can become especially painful and hazardous.

Paper wasps are black, brown, or red with long slender bodies and a narrow waist. Their nests are often round combs of cells that open downward and that are found under eaves of houses, behind shutters, and in shrubs and woodpiles.

Hornets are larger than yellow jackets and honeybees. They are black or brown with white, yellow, or orange markings. Their gray or brown football-shaped nests are found high above the ground on branches of trees or in tree hollows.

Fire ants are reddish brown and are approximately one-eighth of an inch long. Their colonies are built in the ground and can be identified by their prominent mounds. The colonies are generally found along the borders of sidewalks, driveways, and roads.

Using Your Knowledge

Well, okay, you say, now I know my enemy, but what do I do with this knowledge? Knowledge gives you the power to control your behavior in a way that lessens the likelihood of your being stung. The following tips will help you protect yourself:

- Avoid walking barefoot in the grass.

- Do not rely on insect repellents as they do not work against stinging insects.

- Avoid wearing bright-colored clothing with flowery patterns.

- Avoid wearing sweet-smelling perfumes, hairsprays, colognes, and deodorants.

- Never swat or flail at a stinging insect; move away quietly or wait patiently for it to go.

- Cover garbage cans with tight-fitting lids.

- Drink cautiously from open beverage cans and bottles. When eating outside, keep food covered at all times.

- Inspect the home and yard weekly for new hives or nests, especially in the spring, summer, and fall.

- Watch out for nests in trees, shrubs, woodpiles, under eaves of houses, and under rotted wood in gardens and wooded areas.

What if I Am Stung?

Since most people are not allergic to insect stings, you need to recognize the difference between an allergic reaction to a sting, a normal local reaction, and a large local reaction. In all cases, the first thing to do is not to panic.

The normal nonallergic reactions to stings vary, depending on the person and where on the body the sting is. A normal reaction results in pain, swelling, and redness confined to the sting site. Stings on the palms of the hands or between the fingers, on the soles of the feet or between the toes, or on the forehead or temples frequently result in swelling of the tops of the hands and fingers, feet and toes, or eyelids. Although these reactions are very uncomfortable, they are expected and are not usually significant allergic reactions. After removing any remaining stinger (in the case of a honeybee sting), you should simply disinfect the area and apply ice to the area. Antihistamines may be helpful.

Large local reactions are those that extend well beyond the sting site. Swelling at the site of a sting on the forearm may extend to the wrist and elbow and may persist for two to three days. These large reactions are treated the same as normal reactions, although doctors will frequently add antihistamines and sometimes even steroids to the therapy. Even if you have a large local reaction, it does not mean that the next time you are stung you will have an allergic reaction.

Allergic reactions are also called systemic anaphylactic reactions because parts of the body, other than the place where the sting has occurred, are affected immediately, within minutes. Again, the signs and symptoms are:

- Hives, itching, flushing, or swelling in areas other than the sting site

- Tightness in the chest and difficulty breathing

- Hoarse voice or swelling of the tongue

- Nausea, vomiting, abdominal cramps, or diarrhea

- Dizziness and a sharp fall in blood pressure

- Unconsciousness or cardiac arrest

It is much easier to prevent an allergic systemic anaphylactic reaction than to have to treat one. But then again, accidents do happen all the time, despite a person's best efforts to avoid being stung. In that case, if you happen to be allergic to insect stings and you are stung, you need to be prepared to give yourself emergency treatment and then get to a hospital emergency room for further treatment and observation, if necessary.

If you have experienced an allergic reaction to a sting, the first thing you need to do is to see a doctor for a follow-up program. Your doctor will probably prescribe a syringe device that will allow you to self-administer (inject) epinephrine (adrenaline). You need to do this immediately if you are stung and have any symptoms other than at the site of the sting. Do not wait until you feel sick. Adrenaline will prevent an anaphylactic reaction. However, because its effects last only about thirty minutes, you must still seek immediate medical care, at a hospital emergency room. The reaction can return, and it can be just as serious.

In the hospital emergency room, you may be treated with intravenous fluids, oxygen, antihistamines, and steroids, depending upon the severity of your reaction. This is almost always effective. Failures occur when epinephrine is not administered early and there is a delay in seeking medical attention. Remember, you should carry your adrenaline self-administering device with you or have it nearby at all times.

Venom Immunotherapy

At some point in mathematics classes, you should learn about statistics and probability—what gamblers call "the odds." The odds, or risk, of someone having an allergic reaction to an insect sting are less than 5 percent. But for people who have had an allergic reaction to insect stings, the odds of having a similar or worse reaction if stung again are between 60 percent and 100 percent—reason enough to always carry an epinephrine device with you.

It is also reason enough to consider allergen immunotherapy injections with stinging insect venom vaccines. These "shots" are 97 percent effective in preventing future occurrences. The hyposensitization program consists of weekly injections by a physician of increasing amounts of the venoms to which you are sensitive, as determined by allergy skin tests. After fifteen weeks of injections, further shots are given at four- to six-week intervals for another three to five years, depending upon your response as measured by skin tests at reevaluation office visits to your allergist. After the fifteen-week buildup period, you will be able to completely tolerate one or two insect stings, which is equivalent to the amount of venom in the top dose of the injection series. The high risk of anaphylaxis can thus be virtually eliminated.

Food Allergies

Are you one of those people who does not like spinach or broccoli? Do your parents still remind you that Popeye the Sailor Man developed bulging muscles when he ate spinach or that broccoli prevents heart attacks? Neither your dislike of spinach and broccoli nor Popeye's cravings for spinach have anything to do with food allergy. Your particular taste and allergy are two distinctly different things.

On the other hand, does your mouth itch when you eat bananas or melons (or watermelon, honeydew, cantaloupe)? This is a mild allergic reaction. Allergic reactions to foods can range in severity in individuals from an itchy tongue to life-threatening swelling of the throat, asthma, and anaphylactic shock. If you, a family member, or a friend has these problems, then it is important to understand why this happens and how it can best be treated.

History of Food Allergies

It was the Roman philosopher and poet Lucretius (96 to 55 BC) who wrote, "What is food to one man may be fierce poison to others." But the first descriptions of food allergies came even hundreds of years earlier than that. Hippocrates (460 to 377 BC), the Greek physician known as the father of modern medicine, was the first person to report that cow's milk could cause an upset stomach and hives. Hippocrates observed that certain men reacted adversely to cheese (the coagulated casein part of cow's milk). He thought that these individuals, unlike most other men, produced an unusual body substance, or humor, that caused the body to react in this way.

Hippocrates observed, "Cheese does not harm all men alike; some can eat their fill of it without the slightest hurt, nay, those it agrees with are wonderfully strengthened thereby. Others come off badly. So the constitutions of these men differ, and the difference lies in the constituent of the body which is hostile to cheese, and is roused and stirred to action under its influence. Those in whom a humor of such a kind is present in greater quantity, and with greater control over the body naturally suffer more severely. But if cheese were bad for the human constitution without exception, it would have hurt all."

This description is amazingly prophetic, and it remains one of the classic descriptions in the practice of modern allergy. Today, because of developments in the sciences of genetics and immunology, doctors know that the special humor spoken about by Hippocrates is IgE, the class of proteins that trigger allergic reactions not only to food but to other substances.

Allergy vs. Adverse Reaction

Adverse reactions to foods are properly categorized either as food intolerance or food allergy. It is important to distinguish true food allergy from the various other kinds of adverse reactions to food. Most adverse reactions to food are food intolerance reactions. Examples of food intolerance reactions include:

⮑ Common intestinal enzyme deficiencies, such as lactose intolerance

⮑ Other enzyme deficiencies, such as phenylketonuria, galactosemia, or cystic fibrosis

⮑ Food poisoning, such as staphylococcus, salmonella, shigella, or E. coli poisoning

⮑ Other reactions to toxic chemicals, such as botulism, toxic mushrooms, scombroid-fish poisoning

⮑ Psychological reactions, such as food dislikes, food fads, or food aversions, and eating disorders, such as bulimia or anorexia

Food allergy, or hypersensivity, is an abnormal response to a food that is triggered by the immune system, most usually by IgE antibodies reacting with food proteins (allergens). The immune system is not responsible for the symptoms of food intolerance, even though sometimes these symptoms can resemble those of a food allergy.

Food Allergy in Children and Adults

Perhaps you know someone who is allergic to one of the common food allergens, such as cow's milk, egg white, peanuts, tree nuts (filbert, walnut, cashew, pecan, almond, pistachio), or fish or shellfish (shrimp, lobster, crab, oyster, clam).

Milk, egg, and peanut are the most common child-hood food allergies. Allergic sensitivity to tree nuts and shellfish are more common in adulthood. Food allergies commonly begin in the first two years of life and occur in approximately 8 percent of infants. Most children out-grow milk and egg allergies, but allergy to peanuts usu-ally lasts through adulthood and can be lethal. In adult-hood, an additional 1 to 2 percent of the population will develop food allergies.

About 75 percent of infants with eczema (atopic der-matitis) have some degree of allergic sensitization to egg white. One-third of infants with eczema have clinically significant food allergy. One-third of people who are aller-gic to peanuts also are allergic to tree nuts. Many of these people also have asthma.

As you enter adulthood, there are two special types of reactions to food that you may encounter. The first is the "oral allergy syndrome." Symptoms consist of itching, tin-gling, or swelling of the tongue, mouth, or throat that occurs while or immediately after a person eats a certain food.

This reaction usually occurs in some—but not all—people who are allergic to certain pollens and experience a reaction to certain fruits or vegetables. For instance, people with ragweed hay fever may react to bananas and melons. People with birch pollen allergy may not be able to toler-ate apples, carrots, celery, hazelnut, kiwi, pear, or potato. Individuals who are allergic to grass pollen may have trou-ble with celery or peaches. Cooking usually destroys the food allergen responsible for this type of reaction. The rela-tionship of the pollen to the food indicates that they have similar chemical structures—a similarity that the allergic person's immune system recognizes and responds to.

The second type of reaction to food experienced by young adults is "food-dependent, exercise-induced anaphylaxis." This can be very serious, even potentially life-threatening. This reaction is a kind of "double whammy." Eating certain foods and then exercising results in severe hives, wheezing, and even shock. Exercising alone or eating the food without exercising does not cause the problem. The foods most frequently involved are celery, carrots, apples, shrimp, oysters, and chicken. A similar reaction occurs in some people who are allergic to nonsteroidal anti-inflammatory drugs (NSAIDs), such as ibuprofen and aspirin.

Signs and Symptoms

A person who is allergic to a food can experience symptoms from one or more places in their body that are affected by the immune reaction to that food. Reactions can vary in intensity and severity, from being an annoyance or inconvenience to being fatal. An estimated fifty people each year in the United States die from allergic reactions to food. Symptoms can range from an itchy or swollen tongue to swelling of the throat (laryngeal edema) and even anaphylactic shock (difficulty breathing, drop in blood pressure, loss of consciousness). Reactions of the skin include hives (urticaria) and swelling (angioedema). Gastrointestinal reactions include nausea, vomiting, and diarrhea. Other common symptoms involve the respiratory tract: sneezing; nasal congestion; runny nose; itchy, watery, or red eyes (conjunctivitis); and wheezing.

Hows and Whys

The mechanisms by which people become sensitized to foods and subsequently react to them are very similar to the mechanisms that occur in people who are allergic to inhalant allergens, such as cat allergen or ragweed allergen. The difference is that with food allergy, the food allergen enters the body through the cell layer (epithelium) that lines the gastrointestinal tract (mouth, esophagus, stomach, large and small intestines). With respiratory allergy, by contrast, allergens in the air enter the body through the cell layer covering the eye and lining of the upper and lower respiratory tract.

Like other allergies, food allergies are in part inherited. But there are other factors that are just as important in determining whether a person will have the same food allergies as his or her parents. These other factors include:

➱ The age at which a person is first exposed to the food allergen

➱ The amount of food allergen a person is exposed to at the time he or she is sensitized

➱ Whether a person's gastrointestinal epithelial surface barrier can be penetrated by the food allergen

➱ The status of a person's immune system at the time of early exposure to the allergen

As a person's immune system changes, so does his or her chances of developing a food allergy (become sensitized) or outgrowing a food allergy (become tolerant). All foods are potential allergens, although some more so than others. However, most people's immune systems favor tolerance to almost all foods.

Sensitization can occur prior to birth. The developing fetus is nourished by the mother through her blood supply and through the amniotic fluid in the womb. In this way, food allergens can be transferred to the fetus. If the fetus is genetically programmed to develop IgE antibodies to a particular food allergen, it will do so when exposed. This can happen as early as the twentieth week of a fetus's development.

Obviously, what women eat during pregnancy is important. In day-to-day life, it is very difficult to avoid eating such common food sensitizers as milk, egg, and nuts, since these foods are common ingredients in many prepared foods and are frequent hidden ingredients in others. What makes things even more difficult is that it takes only a very small amount of an allergenic food to sensitize a person, especially a fetus that is still developing. An important characteristic of food-allergic people is that they become sensitized by tiny amounts of allergen. After they have become sensitized, they can experience severe allergic reactions to even a tiny amount of the food.

A child can also be sensitized after birth, either by food allergens in its mother's breast milk or by foods that are part of the diet. In a child, the gastrointestinal epithelial lining (mucosa) does not mature until the end of the first year. Before this happens, intact food allergens in incompletely digested foods can penetrate what eventually becomes a gastrointestinal mucosal barrier to food allergens. Below the surface of the intestines are the cells of the immune system, ready to recognize and process the allergen and arm the immune system to react vigorously when it sees that allergen again. The immune system then exerts its influence through the production of mediators, such as histamine, which directly cause sneezing, wheezing, itching, hives, vomiting, diarrhea, and shock.

Controlling Food Allergies

The best way to control food allergies would be to prevent sensitization in the first place. Unfortunately, doctors do not yet know exactly how to prevent sensitization.

But once a person has been sensitized, there is one way to prevent an allergic reaction: Recognize what foods you are allergic to and avoid eating them. This principal of allergy control is called "avoidance" when applied to food allergy and "environmental control" when applied to inhalant allergy. If you can avoid exposing yourself to the allergen to which you have been sensitized, you will not trigger an allergic reaction. For food-allergic people, this means carefully reading the labels of all commercially prepared foods and being aware of situations where food allergens may be hidden in foods. Examples include the presence of cow's milk proteins (whey) in bread and peanuts in Chinese egg rolls.

You should inform your school about the food to which you are allergic. School lunch menus are usually provided several days prior to meals, which allows you to anticipate possible exposures and plan alternative meals or bring your own food from home. Wear a Medic Alert bracelet or necklace. That way, in case of a medical emergency that leaves you unable to communicate clearly, medical personnel will still be aware of your allergy. You should know that even hospitals may not be entirely safe for the food-allergic patient. You and your family need to inform and reinform every doctor, nurse, aid, dietitian, secretary, intern, and resident of your specific food allergy. Even at the very best hospitals, mistakes can be made. Your continuing active participation in the care you receive is very important.

Besides avoidance, there is a second method of control an allergic person should practice. If you are allergic to a certain food, you need to be prepared to immediately treat an allergic reaction if an accidental exposure occurs. This means swallowing an antihistamine medicine as soon as any symptom appears and immediately self-administering an injection of epinephrine (adrenaline) if symptoms worsen. These injections can save your life, but their effects last for only a half hour, so it is important that you get to a hospital emergency room as soon as possible.

An epinephrine injection syringe needs to be prescribed for you by a doctor. It is important that your doctor, a nurse, or a pharmacist demonstrates for you how to use it and that you practice using a demonstrator device. You will then feel more confident about being able to treat yourself. And remember, an epinephrine syringe at home in your medicine cabinet is not going to help you if you have a reaction at McDonalds, so you need to carry it with you. An extra one should be kept for you at your school by the school nurse. Studies have shown that a majority of lethal allergic food reactions took place at school. A second common risk factor for a lethal reaction was a delay in using epinephrine.

The third aspect of management or control concerns what you eat to replace the food to which you are allergic. For an allergic young adult, avoiding peanuts may not be all that great an inconvenience, but an infant, for example, depends on milk formulas for nutrition and to grow, which makes milk allergy a serious problem. Fortunately, alternative formulas are available. Most of these are prepared from soybeans or rice. Others are actually prepared from cow's milk that has been treated with enzymes (hydrolyzed), which makes them less allergenic (hypoallergenic).

Unfortunately, highly allergic children may be sensitive to even these special formulas. Such children need non-allergenic, essential ingredient formulas, which can be quite expensive. Although you may hear some people propose goat's milk as an alternative, goat's milk is not safe for the person with cow's milk allergy. Finally, anyone who is still growing—infant, child, or adolescent—needs a certain amount of calcium in their diet for bone growth. For the young adult, this is 1200 to 1500 milligrams of calcium per day. Most people get calcium in their diet from milk, but this not possible for someone with milk allergy. For the best health, a person allergic to milk needs daily dietary supplements of calcium in orange juice or in pill form.

The fourth point of management or control is for you to act realistically and knowledgeably about whether you have outgrown your food allergy. It is very tempting to think you have and to want to experiment a little by eating the food. Don't do it! Although most children outgrow allergies to milk, egg, and citrus, other food allergies—peanuts, tree nuts, shellfish, and others—persist through life.

If you think your food allergy is getting milder or no longer is present, consult an allergist before experimenting with your diet. Using skin or blood tests, the doctor can assess your current level of allergy and estimate the likelihood of your having a reaction. If the allergist believes that you are no longer allergic, he or she might want you to eat a small amount of the food under observation in the doctor's office, a procedure that doctors call a challenge. If you are now able to eat the food to which you previously reacted, you have developed what is called "immunologic tolerance."

Immunologic Tolerance

Physicians do not completely understand why some children "outgrow" (become tolerant of) their food allergy. This question is a very hot topic for research because a better understanding of the process might enable scientists to develop therapies to "turn off" food allergy.

Today, doctors believe that the process involves at least two mechanisms in the body. The first is the development of an intestinal mucosal barrier, which does not allow intact food allergens to penetrate into the deeper tissues, where they can react with the cells of the immune system that orchestrate the production of specific allergy antibodies. The second mechanism probably involves changes in the function of the immune system cells themselves.

With inhalant allergens, allergy shots can be used to affect this second mechanism in a way that reduces a person's sensitivity. Unfortunately, allergy shots cannot yet be used for this purpose in food allergy because the available food allergens produce severe allergic reactions when injected. Scientists are working, however, to make food allergens for injection in a program of allergen immunotherapy.

Another approach that holds promise is to find a way to directly reduce the amount of circulating specific IgE. If this can be done, the amount of histamine released will also be reduced and any allergic reaction will either be greatly minimized or even nonexistent. Scientists have developed antibodies to IgE that when injected into people effectively remove all specfic IgE from circulation in the body. It is even possible that by the time you read this, such treatment will be available for allergy patients. In the meantime, the best advice remains "Don't eat the food to which you are allergic!" and "Carry an epinephrine syringe with you at all times and know how to use it!"

Skin Allergies

If sneezing and wheezing are the hallmarks of respiratory allergies, then itching and scratching are the major signs of skin, or cutaneous, allergies. By this time in your life, you may have experienced at least one of these conditions. They are urticaria (hives), angioedema (swelling of the skin), atopic dermatitis (childhood eczema), and contact dermatitis (poison ivy and sensitivity to nickel).

Urticaria

What doctors call urticaria, people who have had them usually refer to as hives. After all, no one looks in the mirror and screams, "Oh my god, I'm covered with urticaria!"

Urticaria are itchy (pruritic), round swellings (wheals) surrounded by a red rim (erythema) that occur on the surface of the skin (superficial) either as a single (solitary) spot (lesion) at one place (localized) on the body or as numerous (multiple) spots occurring all over (generalized) the body. Are they like mosquito bites and bee stings? Yes, exactly! When such swelling is not on the surface but in the deeper tissue of the skin (the dermis), both the swelling and the condition that causes it are referred to as angioedema.

About 15 percent of the general population will experience urticaria/angioedema. Approximately 49 percent of patients have urticaria and angioedema together, while 40 percent experience only urticaria and 11 percent only angioedema. Females between 10 and 50 years of age have an increased chance of developing recurrent urticaria. When hives or crops of hives occur suddenly, frequently, or daily for less than six weeks, doctors refer to this condition as acute urticaria. When episodes occur frequently or daily for more than six weeks, then the condition is considered to be chronic.

Hives: How and Why

If you were to obtain a tiny amount of histamine from a medicine bottle and inject it into the top layer of your skin (the epidermis), a very itchy hive would appear at the injection spot within five to ten minutes. (Unless, of course, you were also using medication that contained antihistamines.) This is almost exactly what happens when hives suddenly appear by themselves on your skin, except that in this case the histamine comes from certain cells, known as mast cells, within your own body and not from a bottle.

The histamine causes a three-part reaction, known as the triple response of Lewis, to take place. First, histamine causes narrow blood vessels to become wider, a process known as vasodilation. As a result, fluid, mainly water, from the liquid part of the blood, which is known as plasma, leaks through spaces between cells in the blood vessel walls into the surrounding tissue. This results in the swelling characteristic of a hive or angioedema.

Second, histamine stimulates nerves in the blood vessels in the surrounding skin, causing them to widen, or dilate, thereby increasing blood flow to that area of the skin. This results in the surrounding redness known as serythema.

The last element of the triple response of Lewis is that histamine stimulates sensory nerve endings in the skin, which communicates an itching sensation to your brain. So histamine is very important, but so is its source in the body, the mast cells.

Mast Cells

Mast cells are special cells that surround the blood vessels in most tissues of the body. They contain packets of histamine and histamine-like substances that are dumped or released into the surrounding tissue when these cells are stimulated or disturbed. The result is hives!

A person with too many mast cells may have frequent hives. This condition is called mastocytosis. When the mast cells repetitively release histamine, pigment-forming cells in the skin, which are called melanocytes, may be stimulated, resulting in brown spots and a condition known as urticaria pigmentosa. Without mast cells, there can be no hives.

Histamine Release

So what causes mast cells to release histamine? There are two different kinds of processes that trigger the activation of mast cells and the release of histamine and other histamine-like chemicals:

➪ IgE-dependent mechanism (allergic triggers)

➪ Non-IgE-dependent mechanism (nonallergic triggers)

IgE antibodies, you may recall, are produced by the immune system of allergic people. One end of these IgE antibodies attaches to, or sensitizes, the surface (also known as the cell membrane) of mast cells. The other end of an IgE antibody, which is the part that recognizes the antigen, which in this case is an allergen, waits for them to come. When allergen exposure occurs, the allergens bind to the free ends of IgE antibodies. This attachment disturbs the cell membrane of the mast cell, and it dumps out packets of histamine. Thus, this process is both IgE-dependent and allergen-specific. In sensitive individuals, it is the mechanism responsible for allergic urticaria and angioedema reactions to foods, drugs, stinging insects, and skin contact with animal danders and inhalant allergens. These are the common allergic triggers of hives.

Non-IgE-dependent, nonallergic mediated hives and angioedema involve the activity of the mast cells but not IgE. There are a number of physical conditions and other chemicals that stimulate or trigger the mast cells directly. The most common condition, which is called dermatographism, occurs in about 5 percent of the population. *Dermato* refers to the skin, and *graph* refers to writing; you can "write" on the skin of a person with dermatographism by gently stroking the skin with a blunt pointed object. The "writing" then appears in the form of an itchy hive. So people with dermatographism need to refrain from scratching or picking at their skin because such activity brings out hives. Dermatographism can be managed with over-the-counter antihistamines. Because dry skin is itchy skin, proper hydration of the skin, by drinking enough water and lubricating the skin with lotions and creams, will help prevent itching.

There are also other urticarial conditions that occur in people whose mast cells are more fragile and more apt to dump histamine than the mast cells of other people. These conditions are called the physical urticarias because different types of physical stimuli trigger the release of histamine. These conditions are:

➭ Cold urticaria and angioedema, which are triggered by cold air, swimming pools, and cold beverages

➭ Cholinergic urticaria, which is triggered by heat, sweating, exercise, and stress

➭ Vibratory urticaria, which is triggered by playing the trumpet, jackhammers, motorcycles

➭ Aquagenic urticaria, which is triggered by water touching the skin

➭ Solar urticaria, which is triggered by exposure to sunlight

In addition, certain chemicals and medicines can stimulate mast cells directly, without the need for IgE. These are:

➭ Intravenously administered contrast media used for X ray studies

➭ Opiates, such as morphine or codeine

➭ Certain antibiotics, such as colymycin or polymyxin

Are Urticaria or Angioedema Inherited?

There seems to be some hereditary component to all of the above conditions since they sometimes occur in several members of the same family. However, it is also true that more often than not family members do not share these conditions.

One condition that is definitely inherited is hereditary angioedema. It can be transmitted by either a mother or father to their offspring by a dominant defective gene that produces either a very low amount of an important blood protein or an abnormally functioning protein that under normal circumstances would regulate the production of other blood components that maintain the integrity of blood vessel walls. When there is a deficiency in this regulatory protein, which is known as C1-esterase inhibitor, fluid leaks from the blood vessels, causing tissue to swell.

Although this condition is present from birth, it becomes more apparent in later childhood and adolescence, when attacks of swelling, precipitated by physical trauma and viral infections, can affect and obstruct the trachea and bronchi. This can result in severe difficulty in breathing and, in the most severe cases, death.

When such swelling occurs in the gastrointestinal tract, the patient experiences severe abdominal pain, or colic. Such swelling can also take place in the tissues of the face, leading to a somewhat grotesque appearance that can be very upsetting. Fortunately, this condition today can be treated and prevented with protein replacement therapy, which is normal C1-esterase inhibitor administered intravenously.

Interestingly, hives are not a part of hereditary urticaria,

and the swelling does not itch. If you have hives and neither your mother nor your father have had attacks of
swelling, it is very unlikely that you have hereditary
angioedema, and your children most likely will not have it,
either. However—and there is always a "however"—the
condition can be acquired, occurring in patients with can-
cers and certain autoimmune conditions, such as systemic
lupus erythematosus (SLE).

Confused? That's understandable, but you do not have
to remain that way. If you are concerned about having
urticaria, angioedema, or hereditary angioedema, make
an appointment with your doctor or ask your doctor to
refer you to an allergist. A properly trained physician can
reach a diagnosis by taking a history and, in special circumstances, by doing special blood tests and performing
allergy skin tests.

Hives: What Else Should I Know?

You have already learned that hives can be due to IgE-dependent allergic reactions to foods, drugs, and stings; to non-IgE-
dependent physical stimuli in certain individuals; and to
hereditary factors in certain families. Recurrent and chronic
urticaria and angioedema can also be caused by aspirin and
other nonsteroidal anti-inflammatory drugs (NSAIDs), such as
ibuprofen. It is amazing how frequently people forget they
are taking these medicines for minor headaches, aches, and
pains and never consider that they might be causing their
hives. NSAIDs are enzyme inhibitors that affect the way that
fats are metabolized in the cells, resulting in the release of
histamine-like substances that can cause hives and asthma.

Atopic Dermatitis

The word "dermatitis" is derived from the Latin noun *dermis*, which means skin, and from the suffix *itis*, which means disease or inflammation. The term "atopy" is derived from the Greek word *atopia* and literally means strangeness or strange disease. Allergists use "atopic" to describe a family tendency to develop IgE antibodies and the atopic conditions—atopic dermatitis (eczema), hay fever, and asthma.

Atopic dermatitis (AD) is thus chronic inflammation of the skin that occurs in children who develop IgE antibodies to many allergens and have a tendency to develop hay fever and asthma. AD is commonly called eczema. Ten percent of the childhood population is affected. Most often, it appears in the first year of life: 85 percent of cases are present when a child is between six weeks and five years old. Parents often hope that their children will "outgrow" their AD by age two or three. However, AD persists into later childhood in 70 percent of cases and even into adulthood 20 percent of the time. By the time they reach adulthood, 50 percent of children with AD will have developed asthma and/or hay fever.

What AD Looks and Feels Like

AD itches like crazy! Allergists sometimes say that AD is not the rash that itches but "the itch that rashes." The more you itch, the more you scratch, and the worse the rash gets. If this itch-scratch-itch cycle is interrupted, by covering the skin with clothing, for example, or with a cast over a broken arm, the skin under the covering will almost completely clear. Antihistamines that are antipruritic (anti-itch) are also very helpful in this regard, as are skin creams and lotions that hydrate dry skin. Remember: Dry skin is itchy skin.

When AD begins in a child who is between six weeks and six months old, it is called infantile type. An intensely itchy, red, pimply rash begins on the cheeks and may then spread to the scalp, forehead, body, arms, and legs. Small blisters, oozing, and crusts form. Self-inflicted scratch marks complicate the picture.

When this condition persists in a child beyond six months of age, or begins in a child who is between six months and five years old, it is referred to as childhood type. This is a more chronic dermatitis characterized by dry, scaling, thickened skin (or lichenification) in the creases around the wrists and ankles, behind the knees, or in front of the elbows.

What Makes AD Worse?

Certain situations seem to make AD worse and more difficult to control. These are dry skin, skin irritants, warmth and sweating, stress or emotional upset, infections, and allergens. Proper management of AD entails minimizing or avoiding these factors. Excessive bathing, washing, and the use of drying soaps promote dry skin, which in turn causes itching. Irritants, especially wool clothing, make the skin of AD patients itch. Sweating from hot showers, bathing, sun exposure, and exercising also aggravates skin discomfort. Emotional upset from stress leads to itching, scratching, and skin excoriation. In turn, scratching can lead to infection of the skin, especially the bacterial infection known as *Staphylococcus aureus*. For some unknown reason, these bacteria, which colonize the skin surface of normal people, populate the skin of AD patients in exceptionally high numbers. When the patient scratches the skin, especially with fingernails that are long or dirty, he or she introduces the bacteria into deeper layers of the skin, leading to a staph infection. Infection is a major reason that AD may be difficult to control or become unresponsive to therapy that was initially effective.

What Makes AD an Allergic Condition?

Along with hay fever and allergic asthma, AD is an atopic condition. Atopic individuals tend to produce large amounts of different IgE antibodies. People with hay fever and asthma produce IgE antibodies to inhalant allergens such as tree pollen, grass pollen, weed pollen, and mold spores. By contrast, the immune systems of people with AD produce IgE antibodies mainly to foods, with eggs, soy, milk, peanuts, wheat, and fish being the most common culprits. AD patients also produce IgE to a common bacteria, *Staphylococcus aureus*, and to common indoor allergens, such as dust mites. Sensitization to dust mites is one of the first allergen sensitizations to occur in childhood. The same type of dust mite avoidance measures that are usually advised for people with perennial allergic rhinitis also benefit children with AD.

What Should I Do About AD?

Your primary care physician or allergist can discuss with you the many treatment options available to people with

AD. These include:

☞ Prevention and treatment of dry skin with moisturizers and emollients

☞ Avoidance of skin irritants

☞ Identification and avoidance of potential food allergens and dust mite allergens

☞ Reduction of inflammation with medicines, usually steroid creams and ointments

☞ Treatment of itching with antihistamines

☞ Avoidance and treatment of infection through the practice of skin hygiene and the use of oral antibiotics

☞ Use of newer treatments, such as cyclosporine, Tacrolimus, and interferon-gamma, under the care of a specialist

☞ Ultraviolet B light therapy administered by a dermatologist

Contact Dermatitis

Do your earlobes itch, ooze, and become crusty around your earrings or ear studs? If you answer yes to this question, you are among the unfortunates who are allergic to the metal nickel. Do you break out in an itchy, red rash that blisters, oozes, and crusts one or two days after being in the woods on a camping trip? If so, you are allergic to the oil from the poison ivy plant, the poison sumac plant, or poison oak. In each instance, you have contact dermatitis, an inflammatory skin condition due to an allergen that has come in contact with your skin. Similar reactions can be caused by hair dyes, nail polish, cosmetics, perfumes, shampoos, certain antibiotics used in ointments, and chemicals used in the preparation of plastics, leather, rubber, and latex.

Contact dermatitis is an immune-mediated hypersensitivity (allergic) reaction. In contrast to immediate hypersensitivity reactions to the allergenic proteins in foods, pollens, and insect stings, which occur within a few minutes of exposure to these allergens and require IgE, contact dermatitis reactions are referred to as delayed hypersensitivity reactions. This means that the reaction is mediated not by IgE but by special cells known as T-lymphocytes, which orchestrate a cellular inflammatory reaction in the skin. Because it takes time for inflammatory cells of the body to migrate to the site of contact, the skin lesions of contact dermatitis are delayed reactions. (They usually take one to two days to appear.)

Both immediate and delayed hypersensitivity reactions can occur in the same individual. A good example is latex allergy. Contact dermatitis from latex actually is a reaction to chemicals added to the latex during processing rather than a reaction to the latex itself, which is a sap produced by the rubber tree. The rash looks like red, cracked, blistered, oozing skin. Latex gloves, balloons, rubber bands, pacifiers, baby bottle nipples, condoms, catheters, and dental dams are just a few of the latex products that can cause contact dermatitis. Obviously, a person with latex allergy should avoid contact with latex products. If a rash occurs, you can treat it and relieve the itching with steroid creams and ointments.

Immediate reactions to latex involve IgE antibodies to latex protein allergens. The reactions appear within minutes of exposure and are anaphylactic reactions that range from hives to itchy, watery eyes; runny nose and sneezing; wheezing; and even anaphylactic shock. Deaths due to this type of latex allergy have been reported. Immediate reactions to latex are usually due to mucosal (oral, rectal, and vaginal) or respiratory exposure to latex allergens rather than exposure to skin. Therefore, reactions tend to occur in atopic persons who have had multiple surgeries, dental or medical procedures, and particularly in health care workers. (Doctors, nurses, and other health care workers usually wear latex gloves.) Experts estimate that as many as 17 percent of health care workers who work in hospitals may be allergic to latex.

Precautions include the use of nonlatex (vinyl) gloves, latex-free medical devices, latex-free operating rooms and hospital clinics, and medical identification tags. Treatment includes the use of antihistamines, steroids, and epinephrine. Interestingly, people with this kind of allergy may also be allergic to banana, kiwi, avocado, and chestnuts.

Myths About
Allergies

Perhaps the most common myth about allergies is some variation on the theme of "allergies are not really that bad—just get over it." This myth even inspired a common plot of old television shows: A young boy is housebound with asthma, and sometimes food allergies, too. He looks pale, scrawny, and miserable. Then, with the intervention of some livelier cousins, he decides to just get out and live and leave those inhalers behind.

This myth is one example of the idea that allergies are really a psychological problem, with only a very small physical component. The myth probably got its start when other people saw that allergic people avoided activities and things that made them feel ill. This was more true decades ago, before there were very many good medical treatments for allergic symptoms. Allergic people were sometimes even regarded as neurotic. But it is simply sensible behavior to avoid cats if you have difficulty breathing every time you are around one. Likewise, if shellfish made your throat swell to the point of choking, no doubt you would avoid seafood restaurants.

Allergies are every bit as "real" a disease as arthritis or heart disease. Doctors now have effective treatments that allow people with hay fever and asthma to be as active out-doors as anyone else. But this still does not mean that allergic people can just "buck up" and wish their illnesses away.

For food allergies, the best treatment is food avoidance. Doctors can perform tests to find out more precisely what foods someone is allergic to, so that he or she can enjoy other food items. For example, if someone is allergic to shrimp, does that mean he or she should also avoid lobster or crab? Doctors can do tests to find out the answer to this question. Then the patient might be able to safely enjoy some kinds of shellfish again.

Other Myths

Other myths about allergies are almost as common, and just as misleading. Maybe you have heard some of them.

Short-Haired Pets

"My pet has short hair, so that cannot be what is bothering me." Have you ever heard this one? Pet allergen comes from the skin, saliva, hair, and urine of pets. At one time it was thought that the short-haired varieties of dogs and cats put out less allergen. This is now known to be untrue. Any furred or feathered pet puts out its allergens as long as it is alive.

Some pets do bother some people more than others, and dogs and cats do differ in the amount of allergen they put out. However, this cannot be predicted by length of hair, breed of animal, age of animal, or any other feature.

A similar misconception among poodle fanciers is sometimes expressed as "I don't have a dog, I have a French poodle." Because French poodles do not shed much hair, this has led to the belief that they do not cause allergies in people. Wrong. Poodles are dogs, and they are as capable of causing allergies as German shepherds, golden retrievers, mutts, or any other kind of dog.

Moving Away

With some justification, people sometimes associate their allergies with climate or a specific geographical location. They then decide that they are going to "cure" their allergies by moving away from them.

This is not likely to work. A person could indeed move to a place where the plants are completely different, because the climate is different. The change would have to be dramatic: A person would have to exchange a moist-and-temperate climate for desert, or the desert for a sub-tropical climate, such as Florida. A move from Philadelphia to Tucson perhaps might result in some temporary improvement—in the desert there will be somewhat fewer mold spores.

When the allergic person reaches the new destination, he or she may not be sensitive to the new pollens there at first. But anyone who is allergic in the first place has a tendency to become pollen-sensitive. In two or three years, in many cases, the person's symptoms will return as he or she develops allergic sensitivity to the local pollens. The local mold population may not be that much different from what was left behind. And pets are pets, and roaches are roaches.

Growing Out of It

When children begin to show the signs of allergies, parents sometimes say, "Oh, they'll grow out of it." People often think of "growing out" of allergies in two settings. In the first, a small child has trouble of some sort with a food such as milk, which improves with age. In the second, an older child with hay fever or asthma may have his or her symptoms improve as he or she becomes a teenager or young adult.

Children younger than two can have a number of different problems with food. As they get older, their stomachs and bowels mature and they are able to digest most foods better. Young infants have real troubles with the protein in cow's milk, but they can usually handle substantial amounts after they reach the age of one. Many small children are called "allergic" to a particular food that causes them stomach problems: spitting up, gagging, etc. In such cases, parents sometimes say something like "Johnny can't eat chocolate (or yogurt, tomatoes, tomato sauce, cheese, coconut, bacon, hamburger, etc.) because he is allergic to it. It makes him sick." Needless to say, what Johnny is experiencing in these instances is not an allergic reaction. Some young taste buds and tummies simply cannot handle certain adult foods.

Some infants are milk allergic. Such children experience symptoms such as stomach upset and hives. In milder cases, infant sufferers do seem to outgrow the condition. But the more severe forms, which are characterized by wheezing and even greater distress, usually persist into adulthood and remain fairly severe. It seems that for some people, their bowels and immune system cannot accept milk as good and safe food.

Some small children may have eczema that seems to be caused or worsened by certain foods: eggs, wheat, soybean, and a few others. For most, as they grow out of infancy and their bodies mature, the rash clears. Those with the worst rash often improve a bit but do not clear up completely.

Can children with hay fever or asthma outgrow these conditions? Usually not, at least not completely. Although there are no comprehensive statistics on this point, it seems that many childhood sufferers of hay fever, asthma, or both improve somewhat as they get older. It may be that the hormones released at the onset of puberty, estrogen and testosterone, change our immune systems, resulting in a lessening of allergic symptoms.

Some of the improvement also results from other changes that take place as a child grows up. As they get older, children stop playing on dust mite-filled and moldy carpets. Pets age and die. People move to different dwellings, perhaps ones where pets or cockroaches have never lived. Some children eventually go away to college or the armed forces, where the dormitories are not carpeted and the mattresses have plastic cases around them. All these changes serve as environmental controls, so it is no wonder that many people feel better as young adults than as children.

Food Intolerance

Many people cannot properly digest certain foods. The most common culprits are milk and fatty foods, which give some people diarrhea. This is an example of what is called food intolerance.

The most common form of food intolerance is lactose intolerance, which is when people do not have the ability to digest lactose (milk sugar). In such cases, the bacteria in a person's bowels consumes the lactose and puts out gas and fluid. The result is quite unpleasant. If people with lactose intolerance want to eat and drink dairy products, they can take lactase, the enzyme that normally breaks down milk sugar. Various brands of lactase can be purchased at a pharmacy without a prescription.

Why do fatty foods bothers some people? When fat reaches our stomachs, hormones that increase the motions of the bowels are released. This is the stomach's way of getting the bowels ready for the incoming food. But some people have bowels that are overly sensitive to the hormone, and it triggers diarrhea. The remedy is to eat less fatty food.

Acids

The acids in fruits and vegetables bother a lot of people. Some get heartburn, which is not an allergy. Some feel sore around their lips and mouths, which is also not an allergy. What is happening is that the acid can simply be too irritating for some people to handle comfortably.

Some people, however, get hives on their hands after handling some fruits or vegetables, or their mouth and lips itch and swell after eating them. That is an allergic reaction.

Everyone Has Sinus Problems

Well, this might be true, if you are talking about a frequency of no greater than "now and then." Everyone at least gets the occasional cold—once past the third grade, the average person gets two per year. But colds are not sinus infections, with their prolonged facial discomfort and green nose mucus. Most people, in most years, do not get any sinus infections at all. If you have them repeatedly, there might be something that your doctor can do for you.

Going to the Doctor

If you have always been pretty healthy, and now you have to go to the doctor because of your allergies, you may be annoyed or embarrassed. Most people with allergies wish that they would just go away or that a convenient pill would take care of the problem. But you may have noticed that the over-the-counter pills and capsules (antihistamines and decongestants) leave you sleepy or feeling funny or that they just do not work well enough anymore. And for many people, allergy symptoms are a year-round problem, and taking pills all the time is not practical. So many people of all ages end up visiting their doctors when they are fed up with their allergies.

How to Choose a Good Doctor

Finding the right doctor can be tough. What you want in a doctor is someone who is both knowledgeable and caring. He or she should be someone you can talk with easily. You should not feel that you have to live up to your doctor's expectations; your doctor is there to help you.

You should be comfortable with your doctor. You may already have a family doctor (sometimes referred to as a primary care physician). He or she is probably a family practitioner (a doctor who sees patients of all ages), a pediatrician (a doctor who sees children up to about the age of eighteen), or an internist (a doctor who practices internal, or adult, medicine). You will want someone with whom you can obtain appointments for newly developing problems without too long of a delay—a day or two, perhaps. Many doctors allow interviews: no-charge first visits where you can just talk, which gives you a chance to evaluate whether the physician would be right for you.

Ask about this if you are interested. The only way that you can judge if a doctor is right for you is by talking with him. No doctor is right for everybody, and you should have one you like and trust. Doctors can often tell when their patients are unhappy, even if they do not say so. No one does well in that situation. Speak up if you have a problem or something seems not right.

You can get a sense of a doctor's technical competence by finding out if he or she is board-certified. This means the doctor has had thorough training after medical school, then passed a rigorous test. The American Boards of Family Practice, Pediatrics and Internal Medicine give these tests. Many doctors display these certificates proudly on their office walls. You can ask about this when you call or at your first visit.

A doctor's office should feel right for you, too. The staff should be pleasant and helpful, especially concerning insurance matters. The surroundings should help you feel at ease, not make you feel intimidated, insecure, or afraid. The location should be reasonably convenient for you.

Don't Be Shy

It is perfectly natural to feel shy at the doctor's office. It is probably not a place that you visit a lot. So when you arrive at the office, you may feel a little strange. This is natural. Then you will be asked to sit in a little room (an examination room) and wait for your doctor. Many people find this intimidating. Your doctor will then come in and start to talk with you. In this setting, you may well feel like not talking at all—a common reaction to a new experience. Try to concentrate on what brought you there in the first place. Sometimes people may begin to feel much better in the doctor's office—they are so scared that the symptoms seem just to go away. But allergies do not, so stick with it.

Tell the doctor the entire story of what is wrong, from the beginning. If you forget something, that's okay. Your doctor will also ask questions. Perhaps allergies affect your head, causing headaches; your eyes, with itchiness, tearing, and light sensitivity; your ears, with itching; your nose, with stuffiness, runniness, itching, and sneezing; and your throat, with postnasal drip and constant throat clearing. Go ahead and give your physician the complete list of your symptoms—all of them can be treated and controlled.

Do you wheeze sometimes, or cough so much that you feel like vomiting? Let your doctor know. You really are better off if you find out whether you do in fact have asthma because asthma can be treated and controlled. No one wants to think that they have an illness, but allergic diseases can often be controlled with convenient therapies. Most people find convenient treatment better than acute attacks of illness. Treatment puts you back in control of your life.

Your doctor will talk with you about any other health

problems you may have at the present or have had in the past. Your physician needs to know about any and all of them in order to arrive at a proper diagnosis and devise an appropriate treatment plan. Remember that doctors are ethically and legally bound to confidentiality. This means, that with very few exceptions, they cannot release your medical history to anyone without your written permission (or your parents' permission, if you are legally a minor). Many other illnesses can relate to allergic problems. Sinus problems and ear infections are obvious examples. But many other ailments, such as acquired immune deficiency syndrome (AIDS), cocaine abuse, and ongoing skin diseases, are also important. These may not seem as obviously relevant to an allergy problem, but your doctor needs to know about them.

After taking your medical history, your doctor will examine you. He or she may ask you to undress and put on a paper gown. This allows the physician to examine your chest and hear breathing sounds more easily. He or she may look at your eyes, in your ears, up your nose, and down your throat. The doctor will probably check for swollen lymph glands in your neck and elsewhere, then listen to your lungs. (Doctors examine from the top down because to be thorough it helps to proceed the same way each time.)

If the doctor is worried about sinus problems, you may be sent for sinus X rays. These are quick and painless ways to see if fluid is in your sinuses. Another way to check your sinuses by X ray is with a CT scan. CT scans require more elaborate equipment and cost more than regular X rays. They also need to be scheduled in advance, which means that a doctor usually orders them only when some question of nasal and sinus anatomy or sinus infection cannot be conclusively answered otherwise.

After talking to you and examining you, your doctor will talk with you about what is wrong—your diagnosis—and about what he or she thinks needs to be done. This is a good time to ask questions. The more you ask about your condition and treatment, the better you will understand what needs to be done. The better you understand what has been discussed, the better you will be able to remember how to use whatever medicines your doctor prescribes. Medicines not taken correctly (that is, according to the doctor's orders) are treatments that do not work, so speak right up.

Another reason to ask questions is to make sure that what your doctor recommends is right for you. Only you can really know if this is true. Some medicines are pills, some are sprays that are inhaled. Some need to be used more often than others. Perhaps you would rather use a pill for eye symptoms than an eyedrop—if so, tell your doctor. Your doctor will try to make medication as convenient for you as possible.

After the Visit

Many patients try their treatment for several days. Then, if it works, they stop taking their medication. After all, they are well now, right? Then the symptoms come roaring back. Allergy medications do not work like antibiotics do. They only control symptoms, not the cause of the symptoms. But most allergy patients find that if the medication allows you to feel well, the trade-off—medications for symptoms—is a good one.

But if, over time, the effect of the medication seems to wear off, that's different. What is actually happening is that your allergies or related conditions are becoming worse. That is a good time to give your doctor another call. Perhaps a cold has turned into a sinus infection. In any case, more or different treatment may be needed.

Some people's symptoms do not respond well to commonly used medications. Others find that using allergy treatments year-round is not for them. Your doctor may also wish to get a specialist's opinion. For all these reasons and others, people see allergists.

Allergists

Allergists are pediatricians or internists who have taken at least two years of special training in the care of patients with allergic diseases. All allergists, no matter how they began in medicine, are trained to take care of people of all ages, children and adults. They are educated about the immune system and the ways in which, in some people, it reacts abnormally to things other people's immune systems safely ignore, such as ragweed pollen or dust mites.

Allergists are well versed in the use of medications to treat all sorts of allergic disorders. But they also are trained in ways of testing for allergy to specific things—finding out what exactly you are allergic to, if you really are allergic. Once you and your allergist know that, you can use that knowledge to find ways to help you feel better. When you know what causes your symptoms, you may be able to avoid or limit contact with or exposure to those things. You may be able to receive allergy immunotherapy, or allergy shots, to make you less sensitive to some or all of those things.

Your allergist will begin by talking with you in detail about your symptoms. Seasonal patterns are important: For example, some people experience worse symptoms in the winter, while others feel better. Times of day, whether sinus infections are related to wheezing; sleeping through the night—all these sorts of detail are important. Then your allergist will examine you, much as your family doctor did. The allergist may hold your nostril open with a nasal speculum to get a better look up your nose. (Don't worry—this feels funny, but it doesn't hurt.)

He or she may collect a bit of the mucus from your nose. This is put on a glass slide, then stained. On examination under a microscope, the allergist can see what sort of cells are there, including allergy cells. The more allergy cells, the more likely that you have hay fever.

If you wheeze or cough, the allergist may check how well your air passages work with a lung function test, or spirometry. The results usually can be printed out right away, so you and the allergist will both know the results in minutes.

The allergist may examine your nose and throat with a fiber-optic instrument called a rhinoscope. This is a fine, flexible tube a few millimeters in diameter. Your nose will be sprayed with a decongestant, such as Neosynephrine, to open up swollen nasal passages. Then a numbing medicine, such as those dentists use, will be sprayed (not injected) in your nose. After a few minutes to let the medicines work, the allergist will look up your nose. Today, the rhinoscope is often connected to a video monitor, so both you and the doctor can watch together. He or she will explain to you what you are seeing. This is an excellent way to find out if your nose has a chronic sinus infection or nasal polyps, which often cannot be seen from the front, even with a nasal speculum.

Perhaps the most important thing allergists can do is pin down the causes of your allergies. There are two ways to do this. The best way is through skin testing. Skin testing works best because it is the most accurate method—the fewest true allergies missed, and the fewest false indicators and coincidences missed, too. Tests done on a blood sample (known technically as RAST) have gotten better, but they are still not as accurate as skin tests.

Skin testing can take one or two hours in total, but it is not a particularly unpleasant or uncomfortable experience. The tests can itch, but they usually do not hurt. Based on a number of factors—your symptoms, what part of the country you live in, what animals and insects you may be exposed to—your allergist will determine what you should be tested for. Small extracts of the things you most likely could be allergic to—cat dander or grass pollen, for example—are placed on your skin. The skin is then lightly scratched with a disposable pin or small plastic tool. A hive or itchy wheal at the site is a positive reaction. A positive reaction often indicates an important, strong sensitivity.

If the reaction is negative—no hive or wheal—then an intradermal test will be conducted. A small and narrow needle is used to place a small amount of extract just under your skin. Again, a hive or wheal is a positive reaction. The allergist will decide, based on the size and redness of the hive, whether the hive is a significant positive reaction.

Blood testing is done for those people who cannot have skin testing done. Some medications, especially antihistamines, make skin tests uniformly negative. These medications cannot always be stopped long enough in advance to allow accurate skin testing. Other people may have a skin disease that affects the accuracy of skin tests. And some children tolerate one blood draw better than the whole process of skin testing.

Once you learn what you are allergic to, many new ways to control your allergies will be available to you.

Controlling Allergies and Allergens

Discovering what you are allergic to means gaining the power to do something important with your allergies: control the things around you that cause them. This is one of the main reasons that allergists perform skin testing. Exercising environmental controls can require a great deal of work, both physically and emotionally, so it is not a good idea to spend time and money to change your surroundings unless you know for sure that you have allergic sensitivities you can do something about. In other words, get tested first. Like any other medical treatment, environmental controls should not be used by those who do not need them. (One exception, of course, concerns tobacco smoke, which is poisonous to everyone. Everyone can benefit by limiting their exposure to tobacco smoke.)

Controls for Specific Allergens

Tobacco Smoke

All right, smoke is not technically an allergen—it is an irritant. But it still plays a very important role. Do not smoke, and stay away from tobacco smoke. Do not let anyone smoke near you. (Whether the smoke comes from cigarettes, cigars, or pipes does not really matter—it's all tobacco.) Smokers have no right to make you smell bad and have difficulty breathing. Do not let anyone smoke near little children—they cannot usually get up and leave; they have no choice but to breathe it all in, and their lungs and respiratory systems are not fully developed.

When smokers light up around you, you do not have to sit and suffer. The first thing you can do is politely inform them that smoke bothers your breathing. Do not be surprised if they try to disperse their smoke with one hand, apologize, and give you an annoyed look. You can forbid smoking in your own space, but not in others. So in order to protect your health, you may have to leave. Simply, quietly, without being unnecessarily confrontational, let your host or hostess know that you have to leave because you cannot stand the smoke, and go.

What about marijuana? Aside from the fact that marijuana is illegal, marijuana often harbors molds. So the marijuana smoker often inhales mold spores—not a particularly healthy idea.

Avoiding wood smoke is also a good idea. Fireplaces and wood stoves should be properly ventilated; the room where one is should not become a smokehouse. If you find yourself in a situation where wood smoke is bothering you, go elsewhere.

Cats

An allergy to a pet cat is one of the most common reasons that people get allergy shots. If you have a cat at home, you have cat allergen everywhere: in the air in every room, on your clothes, on your bedding. Cat allergen floats in the air, and it is sticky, so it is on cloth surfaces throughout your home.

Both cat lovers and doctors have tried many ways to control cat allergen: washing cats weekly, automatic door closers, indoor invisible fencing, high-efficiency air filters, and others. It turns out that these make people feel that they ought to feel better—look, I'm doing something about my allergies—but they do not work. Either you have a cat at home, or you don't.

Other Pets

What about dogs? Some people are very sensitive to dog allergen. But overall, dog allergen appears to be a weaker allergen than cat allergen. Dogs should be kept out of the bedroom, and a HEPA filter should be used there. If your bedroom is on a different level of your home from the main living areas, try to train the dog not to go to the bedroom level. If you have hot air heat, get some filter material to cover the vent. Vacuuming is helpful only if you use double-thickness bags that really capture the allergen.

Gerbils, guinea pigs, hamsters, mice, parakeets, parrots, rats, or other furred or feathered, small, caged pets can all cause allergy problems. Again, the simplest thing is to eliminate the pet from your home. If that is not an option, at least move it out of your bedroom. Try to find a new room for it that is well ventilated. Try to stay out of its new room and see if someone else can act as its primary caretaker.

Cockroaches

Vigorous extermination is the key environmental control to practice in regard to roaches. The best way is to treat an entire building all at once with insecticides that kill both living roaches and their eggs. If you live in an apartment, you may have noticed that roaches can return to your apartment from neighboring apartments after you have had extermination done in your own apartment. There is no way to completely prevent this, but some simple things do help. Keep food and water away in closed containers and in refrigerators, where roaches cannot reach them. Do not leave dishes sitting in the sink. Put one of those blue-water things in the back of the toilet so roaches cannot drink that water. Clean up spills quickly and completely.

Pollens

Pollens fill the outdoor air from the spring thaw to the autumn frost. There are a few things you can do to control the amount of pollen in your environment. If your home has central air-conditioning, leave it on, at least in the warm months. If the air inside your home is not exchanged with the air outside, the air inside your home will have much less pollen in it.

In seasons that do not require air-conditioning, leave the windows closed. If the windows and door to your bedroom remain closed, a small HEPA filter will clear pollens and other particles from the air. A nightly shower will wash pollens from your body and keep them off your bedclothes.

Molds

Molds grow everywhere that there is moisture. You can find some mold spores in almost any air sample. But there are a few main indoor sources.

The basement is usually mold central. A dehumidifier is the single best weapon. Use it in the warm weather months, which is the time when basements usually smell and feel the mustiest. The ideal humidity is below 50 percent. This is true not just for the basement but for the whole house— this level of humidity controls molds and dust mites.

The bathroom is the next stop. Television commercials use the term "mildew," but whatever you call it, get rid of it. There are many mildew removers on the market. Throw out that old shower curtain. The kitchen also can be a place where water collects and molds grow. Dry up and clean up whatever you find. Keeping the windows closed and outside air out also keeps out mold spores.

Feathers
If you have allergy skin testing done, you will likely be test-ed for sensitivity to the feathers of chickens, ducks, and geese or a mixture of the three. These are the feathers known as "down" that are used for pillows, bedding, com-forters, and cold-weather clothes. As feathers age, they break down and bits break loose as dust-sized particles. You then inhale this dust. When you are in bed for the night, you have a long time to inhale it.

If you are found to be allergic to feathers, discard your down pillows and bedding, if you have any. Let someone else use your down comforter. But do not worry about down outerwear. You do not really put your face into it, and you do not wear it for that long.

Dust Mites
You can take advantage of these little creatures' sensitiv-ity to temperature and humidity to get rid of them. Think first of controlling them in your bedding because that is where controlling them does the most good. Then, once

you have done that, if you have the resources, move on to the floor and furniture.

The most important site is your bed. Dust mites live in the bedding, which is where you get most of your exposure. First, encase the pillows, mattress, and box spring in dust mite-proof covers. The box spring can be covered in a plastic, mattress-type case, available at any discount store.

You do not, however, want this type of cover for your pillows and mattress. That would be like sleeping on a shower curtain, and you would get sweaty and cold. Instead, consider water-permeable, dust mite-proof cases. These can be found at many "surgical-supply" pharmacies as well as in catalogs of environmental control products, which you can obtain from your allergist. Some large department stores, such as Sears, also carry them. These cases under your pillowcases and sheets comfortably yet completely contain dust mites. All the pillows need to be covered, not just the one you use the most.

Down (feathers) is a good place for mites to breed, and they eat the feathers, too. So use pillows and comforters filled with cotton or polyester.

Everything above the cases—pillowcases, sheets, and blankets—needs to be washed weekly in hot water (more than 130 degrees Fahrenheit). Down comforters can be encased, but it is usually easier to get a polyester-filled comforter and wash it regularly instead. Only hot water kills mites—not cold or warm water or detergents or dryers. A weekly washing of the bedclothes keeps the mite population down. Stuffed animal friends should be of the hot-water-washable variety; if not, put them in the freezer overnight once a week to freeze the mites.

Mites are also present on flooring and furniture. You can use sprays that contain the nontoxic compound tannic acid to destroy the allergen on cloth upholstery. Such sprays are sold under a variety of trade names, including Allersearch ADS.

Spraying may not be all that helpful, though. Most people do not spend much time with their faces on their furniture. And tannic acid sticks to cat allergen, which keeps it from reaching the dust mite allergen.

Wall-to-wall carpet is a great reservoir of dust mites. But adults and older children do not have much "face time" with carpet. For small children, it's a different story because they do crawl and roll around on carpet.

Carpet can be treated with benzyl benzoate powder, which is also nontoxic to people and pets (one brand name is Acarosan). This kills the mites. Tannic acid powder can be used, but it does not kill the mites, only neutralizes the allergen. Carpets need to be treated for dust mites every two months, not every six months as the products advertise. And the dust mite-killing powder needs to be applied overnight, not for just a few hours, no matter what the directions that come with the powder say.

The best way to get rid of the mites is to get rid of the carpet. You can do this if you have hardwood floors underneath. Put rugs down. Some rugs can be washed in hot water—monthly would be often enough to control dust mites. Otherwise rugs can be taken outside and beaten, just as in our great-grandmothers' era. Sunlight kills the mites, cold winter air freezes them, and beating knocks them and their allergen off. Again, monthly is often enough.

Environmental Control Devices and Procedures

HEPA Filters

HEPA stands for High Efficiency Particulate Air. Many allergens are fifteen to fifty microns in size. (A micron is one-thousandth of a millimeter; a millimeter is about one-sixteenth of an inch.) HEPA filters are designed to remove many different sorts of particles that air may contain, including smoke particles.

HEPA filters are available from catalogs, electronics stores, and many other sources. So-called true HEPA filters remove from the air at least 99.97 percent of particles 0.3 microns in diameter or larger. "HEPA-type" or "commercial-grade HEPA" filters remove 85 to 99 percent of particles down to the same size.

Air filters will not solve all of your problems with allergens. Since dust mite allergen is not airborne most of the time, air filters are of limited use in controlling it. Cats put out so much allergen that no filter can keep up. In the winter, hot-air heating systems recirculate indoor air, complete with mold spores and pet allergens. No single-room filter can overcome this—you would need a filter that could clean all the air in the house.

So when can a HEPA filter be helpful? Against pollens and outdoor mold spores. That is, if the filter unit is in your bedroom, with the door and windows closed, it can clean much of the air in that room. (You cannot, however, clean the world.)

Air Cleaning Units

"They make the air smell as fresh as a spring rain." That is

117

a typical advertising pitch for an air cleaning unit. These machines generate ozone, a form of oxygen. This is not the normal form of oxygen that we breathe, but a reactive and mildly toxic form made in nature by lightning—it is what makes the air smell so clean after a thunderstorm. Ozone is also a major component of air pollution (smog). It reacts with our respiratory membranes and is a potent irritant. It makes asthma flare up.

For all of these reasons, air cleaning machines are not useful as a way to control allergens and allergies. In fact, they are more likely to make your problem worse.

Furnace Filters and Duct Cleaning

It makes sense that if you have the air ducts in your heating system cleaned, you should have less dust blowing around your house when you turn the heat on. The same is true for replacement and cleaning of furnace filters. However, no one has ever shown that any of these procedures really makes allergic people feel any better. But if you think it is a good idea, try it once and see.

Humidifiers

Humidifiers have an up- and a downside. On the one hand, when the humidity is below 20 percent, people feel terrible. On the other hand, molds and dust mites thrive at and above 50 percent humidity.

So if you get a humidifier, get a hygrometer, too. A hygrometer is an instrument that measures humidity. Keep the humidity between 20 and 50 percent.

What type of humidifier is best? Avoid the kind that simply sprays a volume of water into the air. It has a reservoir of water that can grow molds, which are then sprayed into the air also.

Some humidifiers boil water into the air. This has the advantage of killing any mold in the water. This type also causes a lot of "white dust," as it puts any minerals that were in the water into the air. They then settle down onto the surroundings.

The best humidifiers boil off a surface film of water, leaving the minerals behind to collect in a pan.

Vacuum Cleaners and Vacuum Cleaner Bags

The type of vacuum cleaner you have does not really matter—you do not need to buy a water-filtered, activated-charcoal-equipped, $500 monster. What matters to your allergies is not the cleaner but the bags that catch the dust. Regular vacuum cleaner bags do not stop any allergens, either pollen-size particles or the bigger dust mite particles, from circulating. The vacuum cleaner bags you want are labeled "double thickness" or "HEPA-type." These are available from a number of companies, including major vacuum cleaner manufacturers.

A simpler solution is to have someone else do the vacuuming with your current machine, ideally with the windows open. You should then stay out of those rooms for half an hour, to let the dust settle.

Medications

When used as directed, medications can provide effective, fast, and safe control of allergies. These include both medications that can be bought over the counter and those that require a doctor's prescription. In this chapter we will discuss each class of allergy medication and what each can be expected to do.

Antihistamines

Most likely, everyone has used an antihistamine at some point. They are used for colds as well as for allergies. Brand names for antihistamines include Allegra, Benadryl, Chlor-Trimeton, Claritin, Zyrtec, and others.

Antihistamines can treat runny nose, postnasal drip and itching. In addition, they treat many allergic eye symptoms: itch, redness, and watering. The older brand of antihistamines, most of which you can now buy over the counter without a doctor's prescription, also make many people sleepy. If you have a cold and cannot sleep or if itchy hives are keeping you awake, drowsiness is good. But if you need to be alert, to drive a car or operate machinery, for example, drowsiness is bad. For about the last ten years, newer antihistamines, which do not make people sleepy, have become available by prescription. A medicine with the trade name of Seldane was the first of these. However, Seldane was not safe when mixed with some other medications, and it is no longer available. As a general rule, it is a good idea to check with your doctor before starting a new medication, to be sure it will safely mix with your old one(s).

As their name suggests, antihistamines block the effect of histamine, which is one of the substances released from allergy cells when they are irritated. Antihistamines are often used quite effectively for hives. They can also be applied to where the disease is, as with prescription antihistamine eyedrops or nasal spray. Some of the older antihistamines are available as skin lotions, but these should be avoided. A patient can develop contact dermatitis to the medication, and then it cannot be used as a pill, either.

If you have problems with sinus infections, your doctor may ask you not to take antihistamines. This is because antihistamines decrease the watery secretions from your nose. This can keep your sinuses from draining properly, which tends to make sinus infections worse.

When allergy symptoms are severe, antihistamines are often not enough. That is because allergy cells release many chemicals besides histamine. This is usually the point when doctors will recommend adding other treatments.

Decongestants

Decongestants also can be taken in two forms: by mouth and by drops and spray. You need to be aware that decongestant nasal sprays and eyedrops can be addicting. If you use them for several days continuously, your nose or eyes may get red and swollen when they wear off and will feel even worse than before you started.

Many people do not know that the eyedrops they use to "get the red out" contain decongestants, but they do. Check the label. Eyedrops that contain only moisturizers or antihistamines are often safe for frequent use. Check for words such as "vasoconstrictor"—that's what decongestants are. A "vasoconstrictor" is a compound that constricts (narrows) blood vessels. With less blood flowing to any area, swelling is reduced. That is all a decongestant does.

Decongestants relieve fewer symptoms that antihistamines, but they act on different ones. Mostly they make your nose less stuffy so you can breathe more easily through it. The most common oral decongestants are pseudoephedrine or phenylpropanolamine.You can buy them separately or in combinations in pills and capsules. Oral decongestants are often very helpful, especially for colds.

Because they share some of the same properties of the hormone adrenaline, oral decongestants can cause side effects in some people. They make some people feel overstimulated, with accompanying jitteriness, palpitations, and sleep disturbances. If used regularly, they can raise blood pressure. Most doctors recommend that they be used intermittently. If you feel like you constantly need a decongestant, you probably need something other than a decongestant.

Steroids

The word "steroid" is used to refer to three large and distinct classes of compounds that our body uses to regulate:

⇀ Inflammation and body chemistry

⇀ Mineral supply

⇀ Gender development and characteristics

The first two classes of steroids are produced in different parts of the adrenal glands. The third class includes those that one most often hears about in the news: estrogen, which doctors prescribe for women after menopause, and androgens, which are also known as anabolic steroids and used—illegally and unhealthily—by athletes to build muscle and body mass. Neither estrogen nor androgens are used by doctors for inflammatory ailments such as allergies or asthma. The kind of steroids that doctors use to treat inflammation are sometimes called "corticosteroids" because they are made in the cortex, or outer layer, of the adrenal glands.

The adrenal glands produce cortisone, which is a natural steroid hormone. Human beings cannot survive without it. Among its many activities, cortisone regulates ongoing inflammation and our immune systems, the amount of sugar in our blood, fat cell growth, and some elements of kidney function.

How much steroid does a human body normally produce? If you had to have your adrenal glands removed, you would have to take some steroid every day for hormone replacement. Doctors prefer to use either prednisone or prednisolone pills for this purpose because they usually have to be taken only once or twice daily. (This is more convenient than cortisone, which usually has to be taken every six hours.) For most people, a treatment of hormone replacement requires about 5 to 7.5 milligrams of prednisone or 4 to 6 mg. of prednisolone daily. When we are under stress, our adrenal glands produce even more steroid—the equivalent of about 30 mg. of prednisone daily.

When used systemically—that is, by pill or injection—steroids are the most powerful and fastest treatment known for the control of inflammation anywhere in the body. The higher the dose, the more effective. In a matter of days, large doses of steroids can bring even severe asthma under control. They also make people feel better in general and often provide a feeling of great energy.

But steroids have negative effects as well. Because they are hormones, they affect systems in the body other than the immune system. They may make people feel better and have more energy, but for some people this effect is too great—they cannot sleep for more than a few hours each night. A person's appetite—particularly for fats and sweets—may increase. Steroids also make fat cells grow, particularly on the face and stomach. More food and more fat cells means people put on weight, often many pounds.

But steroids have the opposite effect on muscle cells—they shrink. For patients who have to take steroids for prolonged periods, this weakness can become a real problem. Steroids also prevent the bowels from absorbing calcium, while they cause the kidneys to release more calcium in the urine. The result is bone loss.

None of these negative side effects should prevent you from taking prednisone if your doctor determines that it is necessary to control your allergies. Your doctor will recommend its use for as short a time as possible, which is crucial. The worst side effects of steroids occur after weeks to months of use, not days.

There are also two "antidotes" to these side effects of steroids. The first is exercise, which reduces fat, builds muscle and bone, and allows you to sleep by causing fatigue. Calcium supplements and a multivitamin that contains vitamin D help to put calcium back into your body.

Inhaled Steroids

Inhaled steroids were developed as a result of the search by doctors to find treatment for allergies and asthma that provided the benefits of steroids without the negative side effects.

Inhaled steroids are the best single class of medications for hay fever and asthma. They are safe, and they work reliably for patients with mild, moderate, and even fairly severe symptoms. They are also fairly convenient, as most need to be used only once or twice daily.

When a doctor mentions the use of a steroid inhaler to a patient, a frequent response is something along the lines of "I want no part of that." The patient may think of bodybuilders and other athletes who abuse anabolic steroids (which are very different from the kind of steroid that controls inflammation and is used to treat allergies). Or the patient may think of someone they know who experienced side effects after taking steroid pills for weeks and months.

The nice thing about steroid inhalers is that they provide a patient with most of the good effects of steroids without the majority of the side effects. This is true because they allow the patient to apply the medicine directly where the disease is: the nose, the lungs, or both.

One thing that everyone should know about inhaled steroids, however, is that they do not work when used "only as needed." Their anti-inflammatory effect builds up over several days. In other words, they need time to work. In this respect, inhaled steroids are like antibiotics. Patients are not supposed to take a capsule or two of penicillin and then stop as soon as they feel better. Antibiotics are prescribed for a specific amount of time, as are inhaled steroids. That is because both of these forms of treatment do not control just the symptoms of a disease, but the disease itself.

Despite their many undeniable benefits, inhaled steroids are not for everyone. People who experience only occasional symptoms may not need to use such medications regularly. Questions? Problems? That is what your doctor is there for.

Cromolyn and Nedocromil

Cromolyn and Nedocromil are also anti-inflammatory medications that can be inhaled. Cromolyn is available by prescription, as either eyedrops or an asthma inhaler, and over the counter as a medicine with the trade name Nasalcrom. Nedocromil is in an asthma inhaler.

Neither of these medications is as strong as inhaled steroids, and they both take a bit longer than steroids to start working. Because they are not absorbed into the body at any dose, they are very safe. For this reason, they are often used with children.

Cromolyn and Nedocromil can also prevent the lung

airways from becoming twitchy when exposed to cold air and exercise. To use them this way, they should be inhaled fifteen to twenty minutes before going out in the cold air or starting exercise. These medicines will not be helpful if used when you are already short of breath.

Bronchodilators

To "bronchodilate" means to dilate, or open up, the bronchi, the breathing passages of the lungs. Bronchodilators are the medications (inhalers and pills) that open up breathing passages fast. They are what you need when you have an asthma attack. The best known of these is albuterol. Bronchodilators are like aspirin for a fever. They work well and fast—and when they wear off, you are back where you started.

One of the main reasons that people with asthma have trouble getting enough air is that when the muscles around the breathing passages become inflamed, they go into spasm. Bronchodilators break the spasm for a little while. If exercise or cold air or a brief exposure to an allergen causes the spasm, bronchodilators may be enough. But if the airways are inflamed constantly, the symptoms will return. That is when an anti-inflammatory inhaler is called for. Inflamed airways do not just spasm; they produce excess mucus, too. Anti-inflammatory inhalers turn off this mucus production, but bronchodilators do not.

Albuterol is available not only as an inhaler but also as pills and syrup. These forms are convenient, especially for small children and others who may have problems with inhalers. The side effects are more pronounced, however.

127

While inhaled forms may make people jittery for a few minutes after use, the forms that are swallowed sometimes make people jittery for hours and can interfere with sleep. Most people prefer the inhaled forms.

Bronchodilator inhalers also provide good protection from asthma attacks triggered by cold and exercise. They should be used fifteen to twenty minutes before the activity that provokes such attacks. The protection they provide usually lasts for two to three hours; use of the medication can be repeated if it seems to be wearing off.

Nonprescription bronchodilators, such as epinephrine, which can be found in Primatene Mist and similar over-the-counter products, have more side effects than albuterol and other prescription symptom relievers. They also do not work nearly as long. If you need a medication to treat asthma attacks, you need to see your doctor.

Spacers

Most asthma inhalers work better when used with devices called spacers. These are plastic chambers that come between you and the inhaler and allow you to get more medicine in your lungs and less in your mouth. If you are using an asthma inhaler, you should also ask your doctor about spacers.

Leukotriene Antagonists

Leukotriene antagonists are a new class of medications for asthma. They come in the form of pills, not inhalers, which is good news for the many people who would rather treat their asthma with pills instead of inhalers. As the name suggests, leukotriene antagonists work by preventing the actions of compounds called leukotrienes. Leukotrienes play a big role in asthma for many asthmatics, although not all.

What this means is that these medications work for some people with asthma, but not others. Because these medications block the actions of only one specific class of compounds, they are not quite as strong at relieving inflammation as steroids. How well they work varies from person to person, and increasing the dosage for a specific patient does not seem to increase their effectiveness. Doctors cannot yet predict who will respond well to leukotriene antagonists. Steroids, by contrast, almost always act to control asthma if the dose is high enough. What patients then have to determine is whether easier breathing is worth the side effects.

Leukotriene antagonists also differ from steroids in that they do not cause side effects in most people. This is not true of steroid pills, antihistamines, decongestants, bronchodilator pills and syrups, and theophylline. One kind of leukotriene antagonist can cause nausea and mild irritation of the liver, and any medicine can occasionally cause rashes. But overall, leukotriene antagonists are very safe medications.

Theophylline

Good old theophylline, which is found in medicines such as Theo-Dur and many others, has been around for decades. It is available as long-acting pills and an elixir (a type of syrup), as well as in nonprescription strengths. For a long time, theophylline was the only pill available for asthma that was not a steroid.

Theophylline is a mild bronchodilator and a mild anti-inflammatory. Although it is better than nothing for asthma, it has some major side effects. Theophylline is related to caffeine and has similar stimulant properties. Even at the correct dose, it often makes people a bit "hyper," as if they had drunk too much coffee. Too much theophylline can also overstimulate the brain, resulting in a seizure. For that reason, doctors must follow blood levels of the medication in patients very carefully. Theophylline can also cause stomach upset and tremor (shaking). If your doctor does prescribe theophylline, take extra care to be certain that you take it exactly as the doctor instructs. An extra dose can cause real problems. Avoid over-the-counter forms of theophylline; this medicine works well only at prescription doses.

Inhaled steroids control asthma better and more safely. Leukotriene antagonists have fewer side effects and are at least as convenient. Inhaled bronchodilators like albuterol (and even albuterol pills) have fewer side effects and work better. So why are we even discussing theophylline?

Theophylline is well known because it has been around so long. Some people have done well on it for decades. Doctors are comfortable using it. Some people cannot use inhalers, for various reasons. For these persons, theophylline meets a need.

Antibiotics

Antibiotics only treat infections caused by bacteria. For allergic people, these infections are most often sinusitis and bronchitis. Because the common cold is caused by a virus, antibiotics are not effective against it. Colds can leave you with ugly yellow stuff running from your nose for several days, but if as you start to feel better the drainage continues to look yellow or green, you might have a sinus infection as well. Colds can also make people cough and wheeze, which can aggravate asthma conditions and require more treatment. If you cough up colored phlegm also, it is definitely time to see the doctor.

Even simple, older antibiotics such as amoxicillin and sulfa medications can be effective if used for a course of treatment that is sufficiently long. So if your doctor prescribes antibiotics for you, be sure to take the medicine for as long as prescribed. If you do not, then you may need another possibly more expensive medication after a second trip to the doctor.

Any antibiotic can cause side effects. Since antibiotics often kill the bacteria that normally live in the bowels, they can cause diarrhea and sometimes nausea, too. Antibiotics can also cause rashes, including hives. Sulfa medications in particular can cause nasty rashes and fevers. If you experience a problem while taking an antibiotic, call your doctor right away. He or she will most likely have you stop taking that particular medication, although another antibiotic may be necessary if the original problem has not cleared up.

Sinus Surgery

For some people who experience frequent sinus headaches and infections, the care of a doctor and an allergist is not enough. Environmental controls, nasal steroids and other medications, and even allergy shots do not work for everyone. For some people, the trouble lies in the bony structure of their nose, and that cannot be changed with any of these treatments.

A rhinoscopy is a procedure in which an allergist or ear, nose, and throat surgeon uses a thin fiber-optic tube, about the size of a piece of spaghetti, to look inside your nose. A doctor might also recommend a CT scan of your sinuses. These procedures allow a physician to understand better the complicated anatomy of a particular nose.

Once a physician has a better understanding of the anatomy of your nose, he or she judges whether surgery to open your sinuses would be helpful. If your nasal septum, the bony wall in the middle of your nose, is greatly deviated (bent to one side or the other), it can be helpful to straighten it. This is because when the septum bulges, it can push the bones on the inside of the nose back over the sinus openings. Straightening the nasal septum allows the narrow side of the nose to be opened.

Allergen Immunotherapy

Allergen immunotherapy is also commonly referred to as "allergy shots" because this method of treatment requires a doctor to inject allergenic material into a patient's arm. The stuff that is injected into the arm is the same as the allergens that are breathed and cause symptoms. In the past, the injection materials—once prepared, sterilized, and standardized for content and potency—were called "allergen extracts." Today, the same materials are referred to as "allergenic vaccines." Since the injection process changes a patient's immune system for the better, doctors refer to the process as "allergen immunotherapy." Because the therapy lowers the level of a patient's sensitivity to the allergen to which he or she is allergic, the process is also sometimes called "hyposensitization."

Allergy shots are very effective, but they are not for everyone. The method used today is very similar to the method used eighty years ago, when this treatment was first developed. Newer, safer, and more effective means of immunotherapy are in the process of being developed.

The History of Allergy Shots

Two English immunologists, Leonard Noon and John Freeman, introduced allergy shots in 1911 as a method of protecting hay fever patients from the effects of "pollen toxin." The treatment worked then, and it has worked since. However, Noon and Freeman thought the benefit was due to the patient's production of an "antitoxin." Scientists now know that the mechanism is more complex than that. However, many of Noon's and Freeman's observations were quite accurate and remain relevant to doctors and patients today. They noted:

- ⇝ Patients with severe symptoms, including asthma, did better than those with only mild symptoms.

- ⇝ Patients with an inherited tendency did better than those without such a tendency.

- ⇝ Age makes no difference to the benefit derived from treatment.

- ⇝ If one year of therapy is completely successful, the protection will carry over to the next year.

- ⇝ If one or two years of therapy is only partially successful, only slight immunity is carried over to the next year.

The next advance in understanding how allergy shots work took place in 1921, when Otto Carl Prausnitz and Heinz Kustner showed that allergic individuals have allergen-specific factors in the blood that they called "reagins." When serum is taken from the blood of an allergic person (donor) and injected into the skin of a nonallergic person (recipient), the recipient's skin then becomes sensitive to the same allergen as the donor. Today, scientists know that these "reagins" are IgE antibodies, which were discovered in 1966 by Kimishige Ishizaka and Teruko Ishizaka. More than thirty years prior to that, in 1935, Charles Cook had established that there were actually two kinds of antibodies to allergens. One kind was the "reagins" produced by allergic individuals. The other was the "blocking antibodies" made by those allergic patients who also received allergy shots.

How Allergy Shots Work

Despite the fact that allergy shots have been used for more than eighty years, we still do not know exactly how they work. However, we do know what happens when they work, and researchers are working to develop even more effective methods of protecting the immune system against developing an allergic response. There is good evidence to indicate that allergy shots do the following:

- Increase IgG (or IgG4) "blocking antibodies"

- Lower IgE production

- Modulate T-cell or mast cell responses toward releasing less histamine

- Change T-cell responses

In short, the evidence suggests that allergy shots shift the balance of a person's immune system from a TH2 profile (the allergic kind) to a TH1 profile (the nonallergic kind).

Who Should Get Allergy Shots?

Anyone who is considering getting allergy shots should first consider all their other options for managing their allergies.

First, you must identify those things to which you are allergic. Some things may be obvious to you—if you sneeze when you are around cats, for example. If it is not that obvious, your physician can help by taking a careful history, or an allergist can perform tests to see if you are making IgE antibodies to dust mite allergen, tree pollen, grass pollen, weed pollen, mold spores, and perhaps even foods.

Once that step has been taken, try to reduce your exposure to the things to which you are sensitive.

If, for whatever reason, you are unable to reduce your exposure, consider using allergy medicines to prevent or treat symptoms.

If these measures do not provide the desired relief, or if the medicines make you feel tired, give you headaches, or upset your stomach, or if you have frequent complications of your allergies, such as sinus infections, pneumonia, or asthma so severe that you require hospital care, then you should discuss allergy shots with your doctor. But remember, the decision to start shots is yours. You need to understand how they work and what to expect from them.

At this time, allergy shots are not effective for treatment of the following:

↪ Eczema (atopic dermatitis)

↪ Food allergy

↪ Food intolerance

⇝ Urticaria (hives)

⇝ Drug allergy

⇝ Migraine headaches

⇝ Latex allergy

⇝ Contact dermatitis allergy to nickel and poison ivy

However, allergy shots are very effective for treatment of the following:

⇝ Stinging insect venom allergy

⇝ Seasonal (hay fever) and perennial allergic rhinitis

⇝ Allergic asthma

Although some scientists remain unconvinced, there is some evidence that allergy shots:

⇝ Decrease the likelihood that children with hay fever will develop asthma

⇝ Increase the likelihood that children will outgrow asthma by adolescence

What to Expect

Allergy shots do not cure allergies. What allergen immunotherapy does is reduce the level of allergy in a patient, a process known as hyposensitization. Allergy shots are considered successful if they result in a patient having fewer and less severe allergic symptoms over time and requiring less or no medicines for relief of symptoms.

Allergen immunotherapy is divided into a buildup phase and a maintenance phase. The buildup phase, which lasts approximately six months, consists of weekly injections, beginning with small amounts of dilute solutions of extracts from the important allergens to which a patient has been proven to be sensitive. These could be tree, grass, or weed pollens, dust mites, mold spores, animal dander from cats or dogs, or venom from stinging insects. Every week to ten days during the buildup phase, the concentration and volume of the injection extract is increased until a maximum tolerated dose or the amount shown to be effective for most people is reached.

This dose is called the "maintenance dose," which is given less frequently during the maintenance phase of allergen immunotherapy, usually once a month for three to five years, by which time most patients will have shown a very favorable response. Once shots are stopped, most patients enjoy a long remission. However, some patients require longer therapy, some may need to restart injections, and a small minority do not respond at all. If a patient decides to start allergen immunotherapy, it is important that he or she be reevaluated at yearly intervals while taking shots and that the patient see an allergist at least once after stopping the therapy.

Are Allergy Shots Safe?

When administered in the office of a board-certified allergist, allergy injections are safe. However, local and systemic reactions to them can occur. For this reason, patients must remain in the allergist's office for twenty to thirty minutes after the injection so that the injection site(s) can be checked and any systemic reaction (sneezing, coughing, wheezing, hives) can be treated promptly. Local reactions usually consist of itching and swelling at the injection site. Application of an ice pack and an oral antihistamine are used to relieve this discomfort.

It is important to know that more dangerous and severe systemic reactions can occur. Although these are extremely rare, they can be life-threatening. Severe reactions are more likely to occur if:

↪ The patient has asthma that is not well under control.

↪ Buildup is close to the top maintenance dose.

↪ Too high a dose is given at the peak of the patient's symptomatic pollen season.

↪ An error is made in the preparation of the injection material.

↪ An error is made in the administration of the injection.

↪ One patient's injection material is mistakenly given to another patient.

As you can see, allergen immunotherapy is a serious process. For this reason, it is best to have the shots administered in the office of a board-certified allergist. Not only is an allergist skilled in the safe administration of effective doses, but the allergist and his or her staff are also trained and prepared to successfully manage local and systemic reactions.

Future Treatments

Scientists in the United States and other parts of the world are currently developing several kinds of new vaccines for use in the treatment of allergies. These include:

- ⮑ Vaccines that do not produce adverse reactions

- ⮑ Vaccines that prevent the development of allergies in children

- ⮑ Vaccines that prevent the progression of allergic conditions (for example, from eczema to hay fever to asthma)

- ⮑ Vaccines that turn off the immunologic mechanism that is responsible for allergies

- ⮑ Vaccines that are given by nasal sprays or by mouth rather than by injection

During your lifetime, in all likelihood, there will be a vaccine that will prevent allergies from occurring at all. Given like the "baby shots" for tetanus, polio, measles, mumps, rubella, and hepatitis, a single shot may be able to protect sensitive people from many different kinds of allergies. This is an exciting prospect not only for you but also for your own children.

Other Hopes for the Future

Besides vaccines, many other advances are being made in the treatment of allergic diseases. Some of the most promising are:

140

Getting Rid of CFCs

CFC is the abbreviation for chlorofluorocarbon. CFCs, such as Freon, are the aerosol propellants that seem to be damaging the ozone layer of our atmosphere. They are used in aerosol sprays, refrigeration and cooling units, cleaning solvents, and in the manufacture of plastic foams. International agreements have been signed to halt their use, but they remain the most common propellants in asthma inhalers and nonwater-based nasal inhalers. When inhaled in small quantities, as from an inhaler, they are nontoxic, tasteless, and odorless. The pharmaceutical industry has been searching for ways to do without CFCs; several CFC-free inhaled-medication "delivery systems" already exist.

For most of the nasal steroids, a water-based, or AQ (as in "aqueous"), version already exists. They have a little pump you use for each dose, so no propellant is needed. More of these AQ versions will be available in the future.

Among the inhaled medications for asthma, the trend is toward "dry-powder" inhalers. These have various fancy names, but their operating principle is the same. You put your lips around the mouthpiece and breathe in deeply. That's it. No propellant is needed; the force of your inhalation draws the medication into your airways. A dry-powder version of albuterol has been on the market for years; some dry-powder inhaled steroids are now on the market also.

Will the "puffers" disappear? No. An alternative propellant, HFA (for hydrofluoroalkane), is now on the market as a propellant for a brand of albuterol and is being tested in steroid inhalers. Alternative propellants could also be used for nasal steroids.

The total number of inhalers (all types of devices) is likely to increase in the future. Not only are new delivery devices forthcoming, but new steroid medications are being tested as well.

New Antihistamines
In the future, more antihistamines will probably become available. In all likelihood, these will not be of the older, sleep-inducing kind. Instead, they will be added members of the existing group of nonsedating, prescription antihistamines, and they should be without harmful interactions when used with other medications. Meanwhile, some of the older nonsedating antihistamines may become available without prescription.

Antiallergy Antibodies
You now know that our bodies make a specific kind, or class, of antibodies against the things to which we are allergic. (This class of antibodies is known as IgE, for immunoglobulin type E). Scientists have now made antibodies to these allergy-antibodies. Treatment with these special antibodies greatly reduces the amount of allergy-antibodies in circulation. What's more, they also seem to reduce allergy symptoms a great deal.

If these antibodies bind to the allergy-antibodies, you might ask, then why do they not set off allergic reactions? It turns out that they do not attach to the allergy-antibodies in the same way as allergens do. So they usually do not trigger allergic reactions. If this kind of treatment turns out to be safe and effective for allergic diseases, it could be a huge step forward.

Improved Allergy Vaccines

Scientists have begun to call allergy shots "allergy vaccines." Their goal is to develop simple injections that would be given every couple of weeks or so but for a duration only of several months, not years. They should be more effective than current allergy shots; side effects from the injections should be reduced.

In one new approach, purified pieces of the allergens are injected. The immune system sees little pieces of proteins differently than big, whole proteins. In many cases, these little pieces of a large protein cause the immune system to decide to ignore (or tolerate) the whole protein. Doctors call this tolerance, as opposed to immunity, wherein the immune system attacks the protein. Current allergy shots induce tolerance, but not as completely as they might, and they can induce allergic reactions, too. Small pieces of allergens, in theory at least, should not induce allergic reactions.

Another approach uses DNA that records the protein structure of allergens. DNA is genetic material that is found in all living cells. DNA specifies the contents of proteins, including allergens. In an amazing discovery, scientist found that if they injected lab animals with DNA that recorded an allergenic protein, the animal became tolerant to that protein! This apparently means that the loose DNA made that protein inside the animal; the animal then treated the protein as its own and so was tolerant to it. Early tests have indicated promising results in humans, too.

In coming years, treatment of all allergic diseases should improve dramatically. In a generation or two, perhaps, allergy may be something we can turn off when it occurs, and "allergies" will be a thing of the past.

Living with
Allergies

However they affect you, allergies are a chronic problem, not an acute one. This means that you have to learn to live with them. You cannot wait until you get better.

Everyone wants to be "normal," which generally seems to mean not too different from other people. Most people do not like to feel strange or different from other people. But allergies do make people different from most other people—those who are not allergic.

A natural response to sickness is fear. "How bad is this, really?" a patient thinks. "Will it get worse? Will it ever go away? How much medicine am I going to have to take? Forever?" Part of this is the instinctive fear of the unknown, which is always scarier than the known. Another part is fear of losing one's health in general, of going from being "well" to being "sick."

One way people try to deal with illness is to deny it and ignore it. "I don't want to have asthma and I'm not going to think about it," they might say. Or, "I don't want to take all those medicines just for my nose." We all use denial as a defense sometimes. But addressing a problem usually gets better results than pretending it does not exist.

People who are ill get angry sometimes. "Why me?" they might think. "I have enough problems already." They may feel that it is not fair that they have to be sick and take medications and go to doctors. Which is true, but not particularly helpful.

Some people feel sad, even depressed, because of the limits they face because of their allergic illness. You might have trouble running or exercising or trouble eating at certain kinds of restaurants with friends.

In fact, a mixture of fear and denial and anger and sadness about learning that you have an allergic disease is normal. Your life has changed in ways you did not choose. Everyone works through this as best as he or she can. Most people never lose all of these feelings. If they did, that just would not be normal. Instead, allergic people have to come to grips with their feelings as best as they can. They need to work to take charge of their health, and this can be hard work indeed. The result can be a feeling of empowerment. This power comes from using your desire to take back control of your life, as best as you can, as motivation to conquer fear, anger, and depression—not by ignoring what is wrong and how it makes you feel, but by bringing it under control the best that you can.

A valuable ally in this effort is your doctor. Many people skip mentioning symptoms to their doctors as part of ignoring and denying their health problems. But doctors cannot read minds. Or a person may not seek out a doctor for help or mention a problem to a physician until it has become so bad that he or she cannot tolerate it anymore. This is counterproductive; if the problem had been addressed earlier, the patient might have been saved a lot of trouble. There is no need to fall into this trap. If you have symptoms, mention them all to your doctor. And seek a doctor's help as soon as you experience any symptoms.

Family members will usually try to be sensitive and to

help, which is not to say that they will always succeed. This means that they need to know what (if any) restrictions you have, but that otherwise you are okay. It is not that you do not want some of Aunt Martha's cookies—but that you cannot eat any food with peanuts in it. Just that little bit of information will keep Aunt Martha from getting her feelings hurt, and both of you will probably feel better.

If a loved one smokes, let him or her know that it cannot be done around you. Let relatives know as much as they need to know, but do not burden them with too much. You have allergies, and so you cannot stay too long because of the cat. That's it; that is all they need to know, and all you have to say. They will be reassured about your basic health when they see that you are well and that you are taking care to avoid what you need to avoid. Only your immediate relatives—parents, brothers, and sisters—and maybe a close friend or two need to know what medication you are taking. That way, should a medical emergency arise, they may be better able to help.

Which brings up another point. You need to know your medications. You cannot be in control of your health if you do not. The very basic level of information you need to know is the names, amount per pill, number of pills or puffs per day, and how often you take them. This may sound simple, but many people do not know these basic facts about medications they have used daily for years.

So go ahead with your life—make controlling your allergies a necessary part of it, but nothing special. Use your inhaler before gym if you need to do so. Bring food to an event if nothing you can safely eat will be served there. Many restaurants restrict or prohibit smoking now and more are sure to in the future. By controlling your allergies, you will see that you are not all that different from others.

Make it your goal to do what you want to do, just as if you had never heard of allergies. This is true in and out of school, including athletics. Bring up your limitations with your doctor—the two of you may be able to find a way to work around them. This is certainly true for sports, where people with asthma were often forced to be spectators rather than participants. A good example of this is the great track-and-field athlete Jackie Joyner-Kersee, who won medals in four different Olympic Games even though she suffered from asthma. If you have exercise-induced asthma, you may be able to prevent it from acting up with a bron-chodilator or cromolyn inhaler. If you must be exposed to a friend's cat because you want to go her house, the reaction in your lungs, nose, or both can also be prevented.

Many schools have rules about their students' use of inhalers. Your doctor can write whatever notes are necessary for you to have access to the medications you use. Do not be shy about asking either the doctor or your school for what you need.

Allergy Resources and Information

Remember: Knowledge gives you the power to control your allergies! One of the worst feelings in the world is to know that you do not feel well and do not know why. To make things worse, when you do not know what is wrong, you do not know what to do about it. The problem with allergies is that everyone thinks they know a lot about them and are very willing to give advice about what to do about them. Sometimes advice is free and sometimes not so free. Advice can be based on anecdotes, tradition, folklore, and quackery or on science and evidence-based medicine. This is not to say that many remedies based on anecdotes, tradition, and folklore do not work, but if you had one chance to pick the best way to treat your illness, you certainly would pick the method that has proved to be safe and effective and to work most of the time.

Therefore, before you chose solutions based on alternatives to medicine, you should start to learn what you can about your allergies from your doctor or pharmacist. The Internet and the World Wide Web can be good sources of medical information even before your doctor's appointment. However, be aware that there are hundreds of sites on the Web that have an ax to grind, a product to sell, and give downright false information.

Be skeptical, be critical, and be selective. Use the Internet to raise questions as well as to answer them. Discuss these questions with your doctor or your allergist. Politely insist that he or she address your concerns. Inform your doctor that you have obtained information from one or more of the professional organizations listed in the back of this book. In this way, you will strengthen your health care partnership with your doctor. These information sources can also recommend support groups in your town or city if you would like to share your experiences with others or learn from them. No, you are not alone. Yes, there are those out there who really care. You need only ask.

Glossary

Adenoids An enlarged mass of tissue at the back of the throat that sometimes obstructs breathing.

Allergens A foreign substance that provokes an immune response by the body.

Allergic fatigue A general feeling of fatigue occurring as a symptom of or result of allergic exposure.

Allergic rhinitis Inflammation of the nasal passages from an allergic reaction.

Allergist A physician who specializes in the treatment of allergies.

Allergy An adverse response by the body's immune system to otherwise harmless substances, such as pollen, mold, animal dander, dust, or food.

Allergy immunotherapy Medical process of desensitizing the body's response to allergens through exposure of progressively larger doses of a specific allergen.

Anaphylaxis A medical emergency that involves an acute systemic allergic reaction (one that affects the entire body).

Androgens Male sex hormones.

Angioedema Swelling.

Antibodies Any of a large number of proteins produced by the immune system in response to specific foreign agents in the body.

Asthma A condition, often caused by an allergic reaction, that is characterized by difficulty breathing accompanied by wheezing, tightness in the chest, and sometimes attacks of gasping or coughing.

Atopic dermatitis Eczema.

Bronchi Minute, thin-walled branches of the bronchial tubes of the lungs.

Bronchitis Inflammation of the bronchi.

Bronchodilators A medicine or drug that relaxes the bronchial muscles, resulting in expansion of the air passages.

Chronic obstructive lung disease Grouping that physicians sometimes use to refer to emphysema and chronic bronchitis.

Cilia Tiny, fingerlike projections that line the sinuses and nasal cavities and "sweep" out mucus and dirt.

Contact dermatitis Poison ivy and sensitivity to nickel.

Corticosteroids Steroids made in the cortex, or outer layer, of the adrenal glands.

Cortisone Natural steroid hormone produced by the adrenal glands.

Cystic fibrosis Common hereditary disease affecting the function of the exocrine glands and characterized by faulty digestion and difficulty breathing.

Dander Minute substance from hair, feathers, or skin.

Dermatographism Skin condition characterized by acute sensitivity that results in itchy hives.

Dermatologist A physician who specializes in the treatment of the skin.

Eczema An inflammation of the skin characterized by redness, itching, and oozing lesions that may become scaly, crusted, or hardened.

Emphysema A disease of the lungs characterized by widening of air spaces and swelling of the walls of the lungs; its symptoms include difficulty in breathing and impaired heart function.

Environmental controls Steps taken to control a person's environment so as to reduce his or her exposure to allergens.

Esophageal reflux Condition in which food leaks back up the windpipe; commonly known as heartburn.

Esophagus A muscular tube from the mouth to the stomach.

Estrogen Any of several sex hormones that stimulate the development of female secondary sex characteristics.

Galactosemia An inherited disorder in which a person is unable to metabolize a certain common sugar.

Hay fever Seasonal allergic rhinitis.

Histamines Group of chemical mediators of inflammation that stimulate the constriction of smooth muscles in the bronchi.

Hives See *Urticaria*.

Lactose A sugar that is present in milk and dairy products.

Leukotrienes Cellular compounds generated by the allergic response.

Mast cells Special cells that surround blood vessels in most tissue of the body; they contain packets of histamine or histamine-like substances that are released when nearby cells are disturbed or irritated.

Mastocytosis Condition in which a person has too many mast cells.

Nasal septum Bony wall that divides the interior of the nose into two nasal cavities.

Nasal speculum Instrument used by a doctor to hold open a nostril while performing a nasal examination.

Otorhinolaryngologist A physician who specializes in the treatment of ear, nose, and throat.

Parasites An organism that lives in, with, or on another living organism.

Phenylketonuria (PKU) An inherited disease characterized by an inability to metabolize a byproduct of the amino acid phenylalanine. Its symptoms include severe mental retardation.

Physical urticarias Any of a number of urticarias triggered by physical stimuli.

Plasma The fluid part of the blood.

Polyp A projecting growth of swollen, overgrown, or tumorous membrane.

Provocation tests Tests used by doctors to diagnose asthma. Patients are asked to inhale low doses of certain chemicals that make the throat spasm. In this way, the doctor is able to measure the degree of irritability of the throat.

Pruritic Itchy.

Reactive airways disease Term sometimes used by physicians to refer to symptoms of wheezing, coughing, and gasping that are not sufficient for a diagnosis of asthma.

Reagins Outdated term once used by scientists to refer to specific substances in the blood that were sensitive to allergens.

Rhinoscope Instrument used for performing a rhinoscopy.

Rhinoscopy Physician's examination of the nasal passages.

Serum Blood from which cells and certain proteins have been removed.

Sinusitis Infection of the sinuses.

Skin testing Method of testing for allergic response by placing small amounts of a potential allergen on the skin and lightly scratching the skin.

Soft palate Soft portion at the back of the roof of the mouth.

Steroids Compounds produced by the body that regulate inflammation, body chemistry, mineral supply, and gender development.

Trachea The main trunk of the system of tubes by which air passes to and from the lungs.

Triple response of Lewis The body's three-part chemical response to the release of histamine.

Turbinates The three small bones that project from the side of the nasal cavity.

Urticaria Allergic disorder, commonly known as hives, characterized by raised, swollen patches of skin and intense itching.

Wheals Round swellings.

Where to Go for Help

Allergy and Asthma Network/ Mothers of Asthmatics
2751 Prosperity Avenue, #150
Fairfax, VA 22031
(800) 878-4403
Web site: www.aanma.org

Allergy and Asthma Rochester Resource Center (AARRC)
360 Perinton Hills Office Park
Fairport, NY 14450
(716) 225-2880
Web site: www.aarrc.com or www.aair.org

American Academy of Allergy, Asthma, and Immunology
611 East Wells Street
Milwaukee, WI 53202
(414) 272-6071
Web site: http://www.aaaai.org

American College of Allergy, Asthma and Immunology (ACAAI)
85 West Algonquin Road
Suite 550
Arlington Heights, IL 60005
(800) 842-7777
Web site: http://www.allergy.mcg.edu

American Lung Association
1740 Broadway
New York, NY 10019
(212) 245-8000
Web site: http://www.lungusa.org

Asthma and Allergy Foundation of America
1125 Fifteenth Street NW, Suite 502
Washington, DC 20005
(202) 466-7643
e-mail: info@aafa.org
Web site: http://www.aafa.org

Asthma, Inc.
4540 Sandpoint Way NE, Suite 200
Seattle, WA 98105
(888) 400-7765 ext. 1
(206) 525-5520
Web site: http://www.asthmainc.com

Food Allergy Network
1040 Eaton Place, #107
Fairfax, VA 22030
(800) 929-4040
www.foodallergy.org

National Institute of Allergy and Infectious Diseases (NIAID)
NIAID Office of Communications and Public Liason
31 Center Drive MSC 2520
Building 31, Room 7A-50
Bethesda, MD 20892-2520
Web site: http://www.niaid.nih.gov

National Jewish Medical and Research Center
1400 Jackson Street
Denver, CO 80206
(800) 222-LUNG

Pollen Counts
(800) 9-POLLEN

For Further Reading

Brostoff, Jonathan. *The Complete Guide to Hayfever: The Latest Research and Techniques for Coping with Hayfever.* Upland, PA: Diane Publishing, 1998.

Edelson, Edward. *Allergies.* New York: Chelsea House, 1991.

Freedman, Michael, Sam Rosenberg, and Cynthia Divino. *Living Well with Asthma.* New York: Guilford Press, 1998.

Health Research Staff. *Asthma, Catarrh, Hayfever and Sinusitus.* Pomeroy, WA: Health Research, 1994.

Hyde, Margaret O. and Elizabeth Forsyth. *Living with Asthma.* New York: Walker and Company, 1995.

Landau, Elaine. *Allergies.* New York: Twenty-First Century Books, 1995.

Murphy, Wendy B. *Asthma (The Millbrook Medical Library).* Brookfield, CT: Millbrook Press, 1998.

Seixas, Judith S. *Allergies: What Are They?* New York: Greenwillow Books, 1991.

Silverstein, Alvin, Virginia Silverstein, and Laura Silverstein Nunn. *Asthma (Diseases and People).* Springfield, NJ: Enslow Publishers, 1997.

Simpson, Carolyn. *Coping with Asthma.* New York: Rosen Publishing Group, 1995.

Simpson, Carolyn. *Everything You Need to Know About Asthma.* New York: Rosen Publishing Group, 1998.

Sussman, Lesley. *Relief From Hay Fever and Other Airborne Allergies.* New York: Dell Publishing, 1992.

Terkel, Susan. *All About Allergies.* New York: Lodestar Books, 1993.

Turner, Roger N. *The Hay Fever Handbook: A Self-Help Program That Works.* San Francisco: Thorsons, 1987.

Youngson, Robert. *Coping Successfully with Hay Fever.* New Brunswick, NJ: Transaction Publishers, 1997.

Index